RICHELIEU

RICHELIEU
(Philippe de Champaigne. *Musée Condé, Chantilly*)

RICHELIEU

BY
KARL FEDERN

WITH TWENTY-SIX ILLUSTRATIONS
AND ONE FACSIMILE

Translated by
BERNARD MIALL

HASKELL HOUSE PUBLISHERS LTD.
Publishers of Scarce Scholarly Books
NEW YORK, N. Y. 10012
1970

First Published 1928

HASKELL HOUSE PUBLISHERS LTD.
Publishers of Scarce Scholarly Books
280 LAFAYETTE STREET
NEW YORK. N. Y. 10012

Library of Congress Catalog Card Number: 72-132440

Standard Book Number 8383-1222-5

Printed in the United States of America

PREFACE

THE purpose of this history of Cardinal Richelieu is to show the living personality of the man—to show it evolving, reacting to and acted on by other personalities—and to portray the conditions in France as he found them and transformed them.

Within such a narrow compass it is not possible to give full particulars of the sources on which this biography is based. It is a remarkable fact that in French literature, apart from works by the Cardinal's contemporaries, there is no biography of Richelieu, and the great work projected by Gabriel Hanotaux has been left uncompleted. On the other hand, there are a great many volumes dealing with individual matters and problems, and these, with Hanotaux' work and Mariéjol's portrait of the man in E. Lavisse's *Histoire de France*, have been largely drawn upon, and especially the works of Avenel, Fagniez, Batiffol, and Magne. Richelieu's letters, reports, memoranda, dispatches, and what not have also, of course, been drawn upon, with his *Political Testament* and the *Brief Relation of the King's Achievements*; as well as the memoirs and sketches by his contempories, Tallement des Reaux, Bassompierre, Monglat, Brienne, Arnaud d'Andilly, Goulas, Montrésor, Fontrailles, Retz, La Rochefoucauld, Motteville, the "Grande Mademoiselle," and others. Little use has been made of Richelieu's so-called *Mémoires*, which, as

RICHELIEU

Louis Bertrand has shown in vol. cxli of the *Revue Historique* (1922), may, indeed, have been written on his initiative, and may in part have been dictated by him, but which are, none the less, a compilation from heterogeneous sources, and revised in an arbitrary fashion by other persons; and hitherto only a very small proportion of the work has been critically sifted and examined.

The German literature concerning Richelieu is very scanty. The best thing as yet written in German is the very perspicacious portrait in Ranke's *Französicher Geschichte der 16 and 17 Jahrhunderts*; but now, after sixty years, during which so many new sources have been discovered, it can no longer be regarded as sufficing. A very thorough work on *Kardinal Richelieu, seine Politik im Elsäss und Lothringen*, by Wilhelm Mommsen, has lately appeared (Berlin, 1922), and this writer has published also a German translation of the *Political Testament*, with a comprehensive introduction; while Willi Andreas, in a volume of collected essays, *Meister der Politik* (Berlin, 1922) has given an excellent account of Richelieu's general activities.

Those readers who are interested in the further development of events in France after Richelieu's death may be referred to the detailed account in my book on Cardinal Mazarin (Munich, 1922).

K. F.

CONTENTS

		PAGE
	PREFACE	5

CHAPTER

I.	THE MONARCHY AND THE ESTATES	13
II.	HENRI IV AND THE REGENCY OF MARIE DE' MEDICI .	33
III.	THE BISHOP OF LUÇON	53
IV.	THE DEATH OF CONCINI	71
V.	LUYNES	84
VI.	THE OLD POLICY	100
VII.	RICHELIEU'S WORK	115
VIII.	THE FIRST BATTLES WITH THE COURT . . .	133
IX.	LA ROCHELLE	149
X.	THE CRISIS	158
XI.	RICHELIEU'S WAR POLICY	180
XII.	THE ADMINISTRATION	195
XIII.	THE DEPOPULATED COURT	207
XIV.	THE HOUSE OF RICHELIEU	222
XV.	THE CONSPIRACY OF CINQ-MARS—THE END . .	233
	INDEX	243

ILLUSTRATIONS

Richelieu . . . . *Frontispiece*	
(Philippe de Champaigne. *Musée Condé, Chantilly*.)	
	FACING PAGE
Paris in the Sixteenth Century	24
(From "*Topographie française*," Claude Chastilion, *Paris, 1641*.)	
Henri IV	34
(Pourbus the Younger. *Louvre, Paris*.)	
Marie de' Medici	40
(Pourbus the Younger. *Ryks Museum, Amsterdam*.)	
Leonora Dori, Marquise d'Ancre	48
(*Pencil drawing by* Dumonstier. *Bibliothèque Nationale, Paris*.)	
François du Plessis, Seigneur de Richelieu . . .	48
(*Sketch in sepia. Bibliothèque Nationale, Paris*.)	
The Duc de Bouillon	56
(*Drawing in red chalk by* Dumonstier. *Bibliothèque Nationale, Paris*.)	
Louis XIII as a Boy	56
(Pourbus the Younger. *Uffizi, Florence*.)	
Concino Concini, Maréchal d'Ancre	80
(*Copper-plate engraving by* Bouttats. *Nationalbibliothek, Vienna*.)	
The Connétable de Luynes	80
(*Pencil drawing. Bibliothèque Nationale, Paris*.)	

RICHELIEU

	FACING PAGE
HENRI II, PRINCE DE CONDÉ	96
(*Copper-plate engraving by* HURET. *Nationalbibliothek, Vienna.*)	
THREE HEADS OF RICHELIEU	120
(PHILIPPE DE CHAMPAIGNE. *British Museum.*)	
LOUIS XIII	128
(PHILIPPE DE CHAMPAIGNE. *Louvre, Paris.*)	
ANNE OF AUSTRIA	136
(RUBENS. *Prado, Madrid.*)	
THE DUKE OF BUCKINGHAM	144
(RUBENS. *Pitti, Florence.*)	
RICHELIEU IN CAVALIER COSTUME	152
(*Copper-plate engraving by* JÉRÔME DAVID. *Nationalbibliothek, Vienna.*)	
LA ROCHELLE	160
(*From* "*Topographie française.*" CLAUDE CHASTILLON, *Paris,* 1641.)	
A COMPANY	160
(*Drawing by* JACQUES CALLOT, *engraved by* ISRAEL. *From* "*Les Misères et les Malheurs de la Guerre,*" *Paris,* 1633. *Albertina, Vienna.*)	
THE MARÉCHAL DE BASSOMPIERRE	176
(*Painter unknown. Versailles.*)	
THE DUC DE MONTMORENCY	176
(*Copper-plate engraving by* MARIETTE. *Nationalbibliothek, Vienna.*)	
FACSIMILE OF A LETTER OF RICHELIEU'S TO THE MARÉCHAL DE MAILLÉ-BRÉZÉ	200
(*Nationalbibliothek, Vienna.*)	

ILLUSTRATIONS

	FACING PAGE
GASTON D'ORLÉANS	216
(VAN DYCK. *Musée Condé, Chantilly*.)	
THE DUCHESSE DE CHEVREUSE	216
(*Copper-plate engraving by* DARET. *Nationalbibliothek, Vienna*.)	
THE PALAIS CARDINAL	224
(*From "Topographia Galliæ," Frankfort-on-Main, circa* 1640.)	
THE MARQUIS DE CINQ-MARS	
(LE NAIN. *Louvre, Paris*.)	
MAZARIN	240
(PHILIPPE DE CHAMPAIGNE. *Portion of painting, Musée Condé, Chantilly*.)	
RICHELIEU	
(PHILIPPE DE CHAMPAIGNE. *Louvre, Paris*.)	

RICHELIEU

CHAPTER I

THE MONARCHY AND THE ESTATES

THE transition from the Middle Ages to the modern period, which in France was accomplished in the sixteenth and seventeenth centuries, was nowhere so swift and so stormy as in that country. The heavily-armed noble, the knight, and the man-at-arms made way for the professional soldier; the feudal seigneur became a courtier; the strongly fortified, fortress-like castles, which but lately, in a century of religious warfare, had constantly to be guarded and defended against sudden attack, were transformed into refined and decorative buildings standing in spacious gardens, in the midst of flower-beds and well-trimmed alleys, enclosed by nothing more substantial than a fence; and a society came into being in which wit and culture united men of very different classes and conditions; while the frequently disrupted State, which had been a mere assemblage of separate provinces, became an organic unity. Many forces conduced to this transformation, many co-operating causes and intellectual currents that were fed from many sources, which, in a thousand ways, difficult to follow, impinged upon men's souls, altering their conceptions imperceptibly from day to day; and these changes were accompanied by grave and bloody political crises and economic revolutions. But whatever forces were operating under the surface and in the background, visibly, and on the stage of history, this change, induced and accomplished by a mighty impulse, was brought to its consummation in France of the Kingdom. Since the old dukes of Francia, the first of the Capets, had taken the field to extend their authority—modest enough in the beginning, and for a time confined to the island city of Paris—they had conquered, and subjugated by a long struggle, full of vicissitudes, but marked by gradual and persistent progress, provinces of the old Empire, fiefs, and independent principalities, or had acquired them by inheritance, marriage, or treaty, and had added territory to territory until they ruled over a genuine kingdom. And this kingdom they retained through the Hundred Years' War with England, who, at that time herself still half French, and seeking to establish herself on the Continent, had held in fee or in dominion the greater part of France. They became what the German kings had never succeeded in becoming—the unifying, ruling, and predominant power. The same house ruled in France for a thousand years—after the elder branch had died out in the collateral lines—and this unbroken legitimacy was of enormous importance in an age when legitimacy, antiquity, and tradition were esteemed above all things. Only once did it appear to be really threatened; in the wars of religion of the sixteenth century another family, the house of Lorraine, in the person of the Guise, seemed on the point of supplanting it on the throne, but

THE MONARCHY AND THE ESTATES

Henri III averted the danger by assassination; and when a year later he himself was murdered, and the Valois line became extinct, Henri IV, one of the most gifted princes of the house which had already produced so many great administrators, succeeded once more in uniting the dismembered land. With him the Bourbon line ascended the throne.

The theory of the constitutional State—which, like all theories, waited on the facts, then, in its turn, to influence the conception of those facts in the minds of the men who dealt with them—was as yet in its infancy. The facts were effective enough in their brutal and material might, but they were, as always, even more effectual as suggestions, as the stuff of faith; and in France the faith in the monarchy was extraordinary.

It was not, as in Spain, a faith in an unbending demigod, who, but rarely visible, sat enthroned and ruling in his vast palaces, behind a rampart of stiff formalities, divorced and remote from the world—a demigod who seemed to the French envoys, when he received them, like a statue that occasionally nodded, or even uttered a few words. The King of France lived like " the first noble of his kingdom," surrounded by a clamorous and gregarious Court, easily accessible, particularly to his nobles and the higher clergy, and even to the Third Estate; to all who had any sort of position in society or filled an office. He was at all times—before the days of Louis XIV—humanly near his people; and none perhaps was so near as Henri IV, the first of the Bourbons, who combined, with his very conscious and authoritative will, a serene cheerfulness, a humane geniality, and a keen, ready wit which won all hearts.

France, moreover, like all the Germanic foundations after the collapse of the Roman Empire, had always been a constitutional State, although a very incomplete one. When the Germans were yet wandering tribes the freemen, the warriors, had elected their duke or king; later, as the Empire became more extensive, and the hierarchy of rank developed, the magnates elected him on the Campus Maii. It was there that they established their laws. Moreover, in the ninth century an elected king reigned in France, *misericordia domini nostri et electione populi*, even though the son was elected to follow the father. One vestige—though not a reminiscence—of the free election of the king survived in the ceremonial of coronation; for even when Louis XIV was crowned at Reims, in the summer of 1654, the Bishop of Soissons—representing the Archbishop of Reims—before crowning the king, asked the assembled lords whether they accepted Louis as their monarch. Five hundred years earlier this question—which on this occasion was answered only by a reverent silence—was one of decisive importance, and had to be answered in the affirmative by the loud acclamation of the assembled magnates and the people. Now the Crown had long been hereditary, while Germany still remained an elective monarchy, the number of whose electors was for ever dwindling.

The theory was in its infancy, but already opinion was swinging to the opposite pole. The authority of the kings of France appeared unlimited; it was, as a matter of fact, limited only by tradition. "We do not

THE MONARCHY AND THE ESTATES

question your absolute power, Sire," said President Guillard to Francis I, "but even if you can do everything you will, yet you ought not to will everything that you can do!" It was expected of the king, his representatives, and officials that they would not infringe the tradition and the laws which, deriving from the Middle Ages, and in harmony with the jurisprudence of the time, consisted for the most part of privileges, of exceptional and special rights, which had come into existence on all sorts of occasions and in all sorts of ways. "We are your subjects, Sire," said the representative of Languedoc to Henri IV, "but we have our privileges!" Moreover, there existed a sort of unfinished framework of a constitution in the shape of the States-General, although these were convoked only at long intervals—intervals of decades and at last of centuries. Assembled for the first time in the year 1302, they had come near to acquiring the importance of the English Parliament during the Hundred Years' War with England; at that time they advanced their claim to be convoked at regular intervals in order to grant supplies; and the principle that the levying of taxation was dependent upon a treaty between the monarch and the Estates, as the representatives of the people, was recognized in the case of the most important of all the direct taxes—the *taille*—in the royal ordinance of 1439. But the power of the Estates declined; even their division into three categories, which so soon disappeared in England, had a paralysing effect; in the year 1484 they were on the point of uniting in a single great assembly, but this was not to be. What crippled them even more was the fact that they did not represent the united realm; a number of provinces had, by treaty or privilege, by acquisition or annexation, retained their own independent assemblies of Estates. In the seventeenth century not only Normandy, Brittany, Dauphiné, Languedoc, and Provence had their own Estates, but also a number of smaller provinces—such as Bigorre, the county of Foix, and others, which had formerly belonged to Navarre, and were united to France only on Henri IV's accession to the throne. At an earlier period they had been even more numerous, and it was before all things their opposition, their provincial "particularism," which made the development of a common Constitution impossible. In the sixteenth century, amidst the tumult of the wars of religion, the States-General were three times convoked; after the death of Henri III the Guises attempted to convoke them; but as unauthorized rebels, which they were in principle, they were unable, although supported by popular favour, to command full recognition of their Estates, and their cause was finally wrecked by the opposition of the Paris Parlement.

The French Parlements, before the great Revolution, were not assemblies representative of the people, but courts of justice: they were, however, courts of justice of a peculiar kind, surrounded by a very different atmosphere from that of our modern courts, and with much more extensive powers. Membership of these Parlements, by a fundamentally vicious procedure, had become more or less hereditary, and they themselves had become corporate bodies, which, in the course of the centuries, by usage, relationship, and intermarriage, had acquired a firm and intimate consistency, and possessed extraordinary rights and privileges. Not without reason the Parlements, together with the Cour des Comptes and the Cour des Aides, were known as the "sovereign Courts"; and before the reign of Louis XIV they implied a severe limitation of the kingly power. Seven provinces—Normandy, Brittany, Provence, Languedoc, Guyenne, Burgundy, and Dauphiné—had their own Parlements; all the rest of France was under the jurisdiction of the Paris Parlement.

In the old days, when the Cité on the Île de la Cité was still the real Paris, the French kings had dwelt there in their palace, and there they convoked their Council—the *curia regis*—and administered justice. In the twelfth century Philip Augustus had the Louvre, the wolves' den beyond the Seine, transformed into a fortress keep, which was originally used as a prison. Gradually the expanding city reached its walls; when the kings made it at first their occasional and then their permanent residence. Francis I commenced the new Renaissance building, which his successor completed in the Baroque style.

Philippe le Bel, since the increasing complexity of State affairs necessitated a certain limitation of spheres, effected a division of his Court into three categories, excepting, of course, his personal attendants and servants. He divided his Council, which from time out of mind every ruler, were he Oriental sultan or feudal prince, had naturally gathered about him, into a Grand Conseil, which was the actual *curia regis* and seat of government; the Cour des Comptes, which was charged with the finances; and the Parlement, which administered the Royal justice. These bodies assembled twice yearly, at Easter and on All Saints' Day; and since for centuries to come the king and his Court moved from place to place, the Parlement went with him. At a later period it became sedentary, and sat in the old palace which St. Louis had built on the Île de la Cité, and which now in very truth became the Palais de Justice; and for a long time the king frequently presided in person—a thing which happened at a later period only on special occasions and for special cause. Originally the great vassals, the prelates, and the great Court dignitaries sat there in judgment, but as time went on they were replaced increasingly by qualified officials. In the seventeenth century the Paris Parlement consisted of the five Chambres des Enquêtes, which in criminal cases had to conduct the preliminary inquiry and prepare the civil process, while the two Chambres des Requêtes gave judgment in privileged cases, in which the Parlement was the court of first instance; the oldest and the highest chamber, the Grand Chambre, which had twenty-five members and eight presidents, functioning as a Court of Appeal. In this chamber all the princes of the Royal house, together with all the spiritual and temporal peers, who once constituted the Parlement, possessed seats and votes. There was also a criminal court, composed of the other chambers and the Chambre des Edictes, for those cases which affected Protestants as such. For special causes full sessions of the combined chambers were convoked. The first president was nominated by the Government;

THE MONARCHY AND THE ESTATES

the other offices were purchasable, as were almost all offices, in spite of the constant financial dearth of the period, the comparative scarcity of money and movable property; at the same time, juridical training and professional status were essential. These officials had extraordinary privileges; they were inviolable and could be tried only by their peers; they went clad in red robes, which in the case of the presidents were trimmed with ermine; when the first president drove to the court he was saluted by the beat of drums and the firing of guns; and the sons of the king addressed him as "Dear Lord and Brother."

In addition to its juridical functions the Parlement had a host of other competences that fell within the province of legislation and administration. It was competent in all that related to the Royal domain, the appanages, and marriage portions of the princes and princesses, the founding of new fiefs, or the granting of patents of nobility; it was responsible also for the control of markets, for foreign policy, for the regulation of hunting and fishing rights, for the superintendence of prisons and hospitals, trade and customs, guilds and corporations, mines, communications, patents, and matters relating to revenue and the coinage. These and other matters were assigned or submitted to the Parlement because it was a council of jurists; and since every legal precedent created customs and rights, even when these were in opposition to other rights and competences, so every problem submitted to the Parlement established a fresh competence. At the same time the Paris Parlement was a sort of State notariate, which had to register the Royal decrees, and because in some circumstances it discussed them and expressed its desire to alter them, it came to appear that the Parlement could refuse to register these decrees, and this refusal became a right. In this way the Parlement acquired the *Droit de Remonstrance*, the right to make representations to the king in opposition to these decrees, and therefore to the policy of the Government. But the king could override such opposition, and enforce registration by appearing and issuing his commands in person. Since on these occasions he sat on a sort of throne-bed, this procedure was known as a *Lit de Justice*. In turbulent periods, if the king was feeble or a minor, if his throne was endangered and he needed the help of the Parlement, the power of the Parlement was augmented; but it declined when the king or his Government was strong.

Besides the Parlements there were numberless lesser courts of justice. At one time it was incumbent upon every seigneur to exercise full jurisdiction within his fief. But the graver cases were increasingly reserved for the Royal jurisdiction, and the land was covered by a network of Royal courts of justice; this was one of the methods of extending the Royal authority, and at the same time of uniting the kingdom. In the sixteenth century the Présidiaux, a species of district court, were established; but by the side of these there survived a number of special tribunals, such as the provostries, the marshals' courts, the "courts of the marble table," and others, which had been established regardlessly, for one reason or another, with conflicting competences; and even the courts of first instance were equally chaotic. But the laws in force were far more confused and intricate than the jurisdiction. A considerable portion of the country, more particularly in the south, was subject to Roman law; a third of the country was under canon law; in the rest of the kingdom innumerable prescriptive laws were current, varying often from commune to commune, and even from street to street. And all these were complicated by personal distinctions, since different laws applied to the nobles, the bourgeoisie, and the clergy. It took an army of jurists to understand and expound all these laws. In the Middle Ages—and as far as the law was concerned they lasted until far into the seventeenth century—men were as contentious as they were formalistic; they took the law violently into their own hands, or entered upon the most involved legal proceedings. The number of those who lived by such proceedings—judges, advocates, notaries, *procureurs*, and clerks—the black-clad hosts of the Basoche [1]—was simply endless. The legal profession had in France attained to a position unknown in any other European country.

Against the power of the great vassals and the insubordination of the nobles the kings—and above all Louis XI—had secured the support of the cities and the bourgeoisie. They chose their councillors and officials from among the clergy and the lawyers, who were more dependent and submissive than the nobles; and the more complicated and comprehensive the affairs of the State and their administration became,

---

[1] Basoche—the ancient guild of clerks from whom the *procureurs* were recruited. It was at one time known as "the kingdom of the Basoche," and yearly elected "a king." Its organization was military in character, and it enjoyed special judiciary rights.—TR.

as a result of the extension and differentiation of all its relations, the greater need it had of trained officials and educated jurists, men who were skilled in writing, and familiar with the Latin tongue, and learned in the law; and more and more, as time went on, the nobles, who derided learning and despised the pen, preferring to wield the sword, were forced to surrender offices and functions to the bourgeoisie.

The princes and the great seigneurs of the realm still sat on the king's council, but already some of the highest offices—those of chancellor and secretary of State—were filled by bourgeois jurists. The governors of the provinces belonged to the high nobility, but, apart from their functions as representatives of the king, their authority was essentially that of military command; the administration, which as yet had not been definitely separated from the judicial power, lay more and more in the hands of the Estates, the Parlements, the many minor officials, the lesser gentry, and the consuls and councillors of the cities. At the head of the provincial administration in the north were the *baillis*, whose authority was for a time almost unlimited, and in the south were the seneschals. As was usual in that age of undefined competences, the officials who wielded such perilous authority were continually associated with new officials who relieved them of some part of their duties, and thereby restricted their functions, until these were little more than honorary. In the sixteenth century the practice arose of sending jurists from the capital—members of the lower chambers of the Parlement—as commissaries, to superintend for a time, and improve, the administration

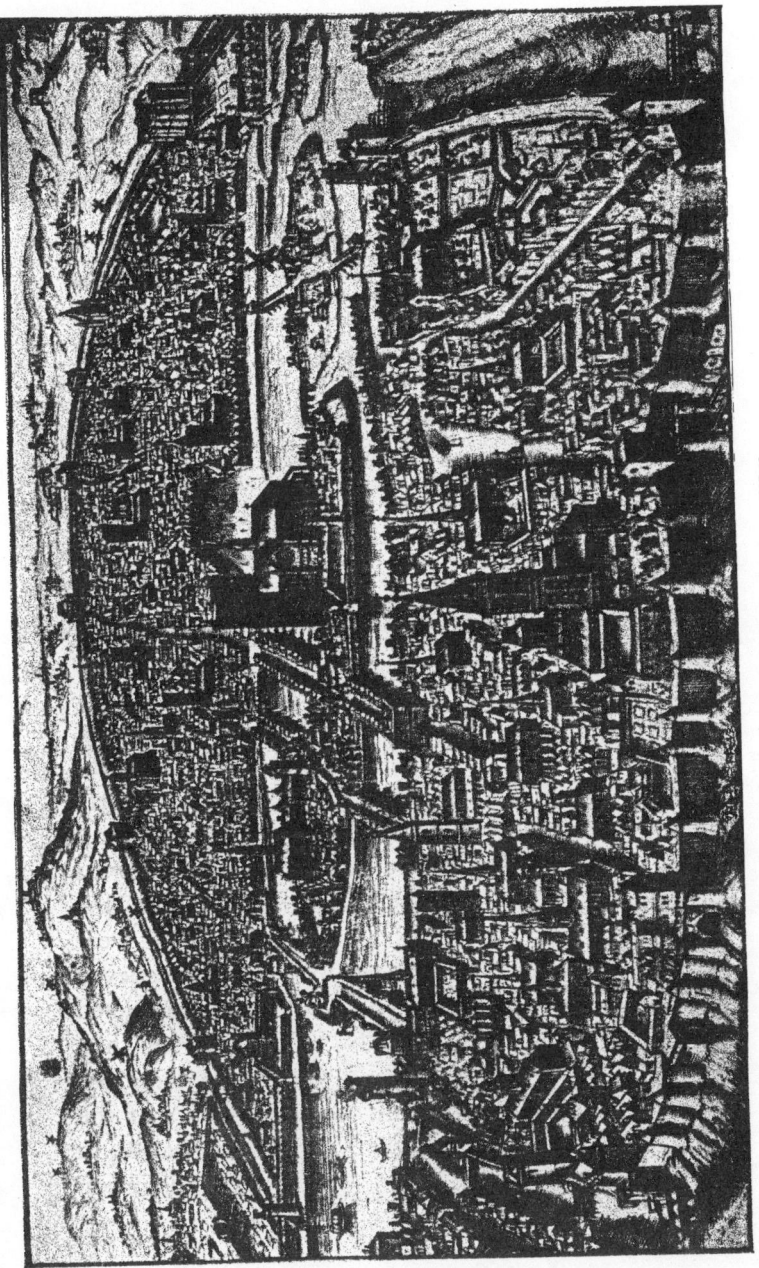

PARIS IN THE SIXTEENTH CENTURY

(From "Topographie française," Claude Chastillon, Paris, 1641)

THE MONARCHY AND THE ESTATES

of the provinces. The administration of the finances was almost entirely in bourgeois hands.

Thus originated the power of the robe. The nobles might fill the military posts; the wealthy bourgeoisie bought the civil appointments. Since the title and position of a councillor of Parlement—and still more those of a president or advocate-general—cost a very large sum, while the return in fees and perquisites was not commensurate, they remained in the possession of the richest families of the realm. In return for a fixed payment, the so-called *Droit Annuel* or *Paulette*, which amounted to a sixtieth of the purchase price, the office of the father was secured to his son. In this way it became hereditary, and its possession was the capital of the family. The system of purchase in itself might be vicious, but the hereditary nature of offices increased the independence and the class-consciousness of the judges. On many occasions they displayed extraordinary courage. The president Achille de Harlay, in the year 1590, fearlessly opposed the Duc de Guise, and two years later the Chevalier d'Aumale, who threatened him sword in hand; the presidents Brisson and Larcher, and the councillor Tardif, during the reign of terror of "the Sixteen" in Paris, were hanged, but did not yield; and the *procureur-général* Molé, in the beleagured Parlement, amidst the furious cries of the Leaguers, refused to change the Salic law and allow Henri IV to be deprived of the throne. Families like the Molés, the Talons, and the Brûlarts became great and famous, and lived for generations, amidst all the pomp of exalted office, in their old narrow houses, a life of bourgeois austerity and simplicity.

Only these "parliamentary" families, who gave the Présidiaux their judges, and the wealthy families of the cities, who furnished the city with its officials—in the sixteenth and seventeenth centuries it was only this restricted upper class that constituted the Third Estate which was represented in the States-General; the great mass of the poorer bourgeoisie, the traders and craftsmen, and the peasants, were either unrepresented, or found only such representatives as voluntarily offered their services. On the other hand, this upper class was constantly pressing into the ranks of the class above it. A title of nobility was attached to a number of offices, and the wealthiest families bought estates which were fiefs, or were created barons, counts, or marquises; and thus originated the *noblesse de robe*, which was an aristocracy at once of office and of wealth. The old nobility of knightly descent looked down contemptuously upon the new; for them the new counts and marquises, the noble lords of "pen and ink," were still of the bourgeoisie; so that the sons of the new nobles aspired after military rank, in order that they might, by their martial achievements, become the equals of the old; while their daughters carried their greedily coveted dowries into the old noble families. So the old nobility and the new, while as classes they were mutually hostile, none the less intermarried and united in parties and coteries, just as the king opposed and weakened the nobles as a class, but at the same time respected them and used them.

By the end of the sixteenth century the old nobility had been destroyed by the wars of religion. The revenue of their estates had greatly diminished, even

THE MONARCHY AND THE ESTATES

before the depreciation of gold which followed the discovery of America, since the rents received from the peasants and farmers had scarcely a fourth of their former purchasing power. After the wars of religion the whole nobility was so deeply in debt that the burden was neither endurable nor redeemable. As after every grievous war, and every domestic catastrophe, there was an extensive transference of property from one class to another. The nobles were forced to sell their estates, and the enriched bourgeois bought them. But the other classes also had suffered severely; individuals only had succeeded in making their fortunes out of the necessities of the times; the peasants were reduced to penury, the towns were impoverished, and the industries destroyed; the French people were compelled to import the ordinary necessities of everyday life, which had formerly been produced in the country, from abroad: the English sold ship-loads of old clothes and shoes in the French ports. But the bourgeois and the peasant were able to work their way up again, whereas the noble saw no opportunity of economic recovery: he himself no longer cultivated his acres—he was not qualified to do so—and in the years of incessant warfare he had lost the taste for sedentary life; he turned to the monarchy, from which he expected employment as an officer or a courtier, and, above all, he wanted a pension—a pension in those days meant an income granted to adherents or persons who had performed meritorious service or had been effectively recommended—and with it favour, advancement, and honours. All but the greater nobles had become completely dependent on the Crown.

RICHELIEU

The great nobles, on the other hand, had rather increased their power in the confusion of the times; the princes of the Royal house and the great feudal seigneurs who were also governors of provinces—the Guises, Bouillons, Nevers, Nogarets, Rohans, Montmorencys, and others—whether they came of ancient and illustrious houses or had risen by recent favour—these men, as leaders of armies and parties, to whom both glory and booty were allotted, who were all so powerful and important that they had to be bought or rewarded, had now become even more important and more powerful, and were sometimes helpful and sometimes dangerous to the Crown.

All things were still medieval; France was still a great and spacious country, covered with perilous forests; the roads were few and bad and unsafe; commercial intercourse and traffic for the most part followed the great rivers; it took many days for an order, an item of news, or an army to travel from the capital to the remoter provinces or the frontier; and distance made men independent. Internal trade and intercourse were everywhere impeded by senseless customs barriers, by lack of uniformity in the laws, and by insecurity; and it constantly happened that the provinces, the walled and fortified towns, or even individual owners of castles, would defy the orders of the king or the governor or the bishop, or the decrees of the courts, and so had to be invaded or besieged and subdued—unless the king or the Government was too weak for such measures and preferred negotiation and an amicable composition.

THE MONARCHY AND THE ESTATES

The lowest of all these classes, the agricultural population, lived a life of hunger, sickness, and ill-usage amid the miseries of war. Since the middle of the sixteenth century wages had constantly diminished, while the necessities of life—housing, clothes, and wood—had grown dearer. All the wealthier classes were exempted from the payment of taxes: " Poverty alone was conceded no ground for exemption." In some districts matters were not so bad; in others the people lived almost like beasts. Here and there savage risings occurred against the landlords, which were followed by bloody suppression. The people, toiling and despised, crushed by taxation, had to bear the burden of their poverty until 1789.

Even the power that united all these turbulent groups and classes, and kept them within bounds, had not emerged unshaken from the wars. In the dreadful and sanguinary conflicts of fanatical groups and armies, conflicts of province with province, city with city, castle with castle, and village with village, all the bonds of Society had been dissolved. Powerful parties had risen against the kings, the clergy had preached against them, great vassals had rebelled against them, and murderers were dispatched to kill them. Since in the stress of the times everyone had to protect himself to the best of his ability, the nobles, the towns, and the parties had chosen their leaders, sought help from outside, organized themselves, and procured money as best they could, and both of the two hostile religious parties impugned the king's right to constrain their conscience. Theory followed upon the facts, and constructed a system out of the necessities of party and caste and the relations and redistributions of the powers involved. Humanism and the study of the classic authors had revived ancient ideals, and had evoked in cultivated men of all countries a certain preference for republican forms and conceptions. Hitherto this preference had been æsthetic and historical, but now it became actual. The Protestants in particular were inclined to this preference. The king, who was seeking to subdue them, was a tyrant; and against tyrants insurrection and dethronement were lawful. The Catholic writers thought and wrote no otherwise as soon as they believed their Church to be threatened. Both parties were united in this—that sovereignty resides in the people, and that the monarch is but their delegate; that the State is more important than the Prince, and that the Estates which represent the people, so soon as the king abuses his delegated authority, may withdraw it from him. In this spirit wrote the Protestants Théodore de Bèze and François de Hotman, the Catholics Étienne de La Boétie, Jean Bodin, and Jean Boucher, and, besides these, a great number of anonymous authors of Latin pamphlets. The Catholics go even farther: not only the people, but also the Roman Church and its supreme head, the Pope, may depose the heretical king and tyrant, and release his subjects from their oath of loyalty; such was the doctrine of the Jesuit Cardinal Bellarmin. And since the tyrant is no longer a legitimate king, he may be killed, but the slayer is not to be regarded as guilty of regicide. The Spaniards Suarez and Mariana declared this openly, as did Boucher and other French authors; Clément and Ravaillac—amongst many

THE MONARCHY AND THE ESTATES

others who failed in their attempt—put their doctrines into practice.

Theory, in the sixteenth century, was unfavourable to monarchy; and even the facts, the distribution of the powers within the State, and the dynamics of the State, seemed equally unfavourable. In the whole of Western Europe the peoples had begun to struggle against the unlimited power of the Crown. In Spain the struggle was already decided, in the early years of the sixteenth century, under Charles V, in favour of the monarchy. The insurrections of the towns, of the *comuneros* in Castile and the guilds in Valencia, had been quickly suppressed. In England and France the struggle was fought to a conclusion in the seventeenth century. The whole of Western Europe stood at the parting of the ways; these led from the disorder of the medieval structure, based on the feudal system and the Estates, which was no longer adequate to the new conditions, to the modern constitutional State, which would permit the existing powers a freer and more reasonable activity and better means of self-defence, or to the absolute monarchy, which sought to solve the new problems, for the time being, by a concentration of power. In England and in France there were movements in both directions simultaneously; and both parties, even if they were not fully conscious of their aim, attempted to force political developments to follow their own path. In England the Parliament and the rights of the nation were victorious; in France, although theory, opinion, and the actual conditions of power seemed favourable to the other side, the monarchy won the day.

But this development was not of the same character in the two countries. In England, where the Norman kings, after the Conquest, possessed and ruled the whole country, the nobles and the burgesses had united against the Crown. In France, where the kings had first of all to conquer their own country, the monarchy and the bourgeoisie were united, as in Spain, against the nobles. The kings employed the bourgeoisie as a weapon, and the nobles, pressed and humiliated, came over to the side of the Crown. Both Estates attempted to form an opposition, but they did so in their weakness and without persistent determination. The natural disposition of the people and many other circumstances contributed to this result; but, above all, personality was the decisive factor; in England the genius of Cromwell was in the van of the revolution; but in France genius was active on the side of the monarchy.

CHAPTER II

HENRI IV AND THE REGENCY OF MARIE DE' MEDICI

HENRI IV had become the king of the dismembered but now reunited land. By his return to the Roman Church he gratified the Catholics; by the Edict of Nantes he reassured the Protestants; by his valour and wit, his geniality and sociability, he won the hearts of the French people. Not all, indeed, were contented, but the majority were so; moreover, men were weary of devastation and bloodshed; the religious fury of the parties had worn itself out and given way to apathy; in many quarters a certain scepticism was apparent; and all good Frenchmen longed for peace. As long ago as 1562 the Chancellor de l'Hôpital had said: "The question is not to determine which is the true religion, but to see how we can live together." Henri IV was an authoritative prince, who had no doubts as to the absolute nature of his power. He did not hesitate to override the opposition of the Estates, and to deprive the cities of their liberties if they opposed his plans or refused his demands. But he was shrewd, clear-sighted, and resolute; he knew how to talk to people, how to handle them; he did not stretch the bow too far; and he was, above all, a man of ardent and kindly nature; the people felt that he had a heart for them and took thought for them. He was grateful to those who served him, and was not vindictive to those who had opposed him. The French of that period, so eager to love and honour their king, had in him a monarch whom they could love and honour. His many and indiscriminate love affairs were not held against him. For more than ten years he kept the peace; the sorely harassed nation had time to recover breath. Bad as conditions might be in many respects, his reign appeared to a later age as the happiest France had known.

His extraordinary personality, his remarkable gifts, were in some degree obscured by his blunt, hearty good nature, as was the wisdom with which he selected his collaborators, whom he liked to treat as his good comrades. He was at once a stern man and a merciful. How long he hesitated before he would take proceedings against the faithless Biron! He warned him, pardoned him, held his hand, until the handsome, foolish marshal made it impossible for him to do so longer, and was beheaded in the courtyard of the Bastille.

The miserable system of finance, under which the greater part of the revenue profited neither king nor State, while the people were crushed by taxation, was reformed by Sully. This ungracious, morose, and conceited person was an excellent accountant and economist. In 1597 the yearly deficit amounted to 18 millions; the State owed, at home and abroad, between two and three hundred millions; but twelve years later, when Henri IV died, a surplus of twelve millions in gold lay in the Arsenal and the coffers of the State, and the burden of taxation had been lightened.

HENRI IV
(Pourbus the Younger, Louvre, Paris)

HENRI IV AND MARIE DE' MEDICI

The foreign policy of Henri IV was determined beforehand. France was practically encircled. In the south was Spain—and Rousillon, to the north of the Pyrenees; in the south-east Milan and Naples, in the east the Franche-Comté of Burgundy, and in the north-east the Netherlands were all Spanish possessions; in Germany reigned the Habsburg Emperor, related to the Spanish rulers, who, by virtue of his possessions in Alsace, impinged upon the French frontier; beyond the ocean lay the American colonies of Spain, which were pouring into the mother country their rivers of gold and silver; the fleets of Spain ruled the seas; she had established harbours on the coast of Tuscany; Genoa, from which she obtained vast loans, was within her sphere of influence; Savoy was dependent on her or allied to her. Since the time of Charles V, since the victories of Charles VIII and Louis XII had been lost on the Italian battlefields to the unconquerable Spanish armies of Pescara and Gonsalvo de Cordova, the French policy had only one aim—to defend itself against the Habsburg ascendancy and the embraces of Spain.

The allies on whom she could set her hopes were the Protestants ruled by German princes, who feared the Habsburgs as greatly as did France, and the Protestants of Holland, Switzerland, and England; a number of small or weak States, against the world power of the house of Habsburg. For that matter, the Protestants were hardly desirable allies for a country in which the great majority of the population were zealous Catholics, and in which the clergy were most highly regarded and possessed great influence. On the other hand, a great part of the French Catholics, whose views were still those of the League, were in favour of an alliance with Spain, because Spain was the foremost Catholic power; the bulk of the French exports went to Spain; and a customs war in the year 1603 and 1604 had proved extremely injurious.

In the year 1598 the peace of Vervins was concluded between France and Spain. In view of the exhaustion of his own country and the power of his adversary Henri IV had every reason to keep the peace; but he knew that while he kept it the Spanish power was continually growing more dangerous. At one time there had been talk of an alliance, such as the Catholic party desired; of a marriage between the two Royal houses (and in those days such a marriage had a far greater political significance than to-day); but the project fell through.

In those years both powers were concerned and disquieted by a mutual difficulty: the convenient connection of the outlying portions of the Habsburg-Spanish territories. Roads ran through Savoy by which the Spanish armies could march upon the Franche-Comté and the Netherlands; through the Valtellina and the Grisons the Alpine passes led from Spanish Milan to the Austrian Tyrol. These, and in particular the Valtellina passes, had been for more than a century the object of endless diplomatic negotiations, and of bloody battles. France could easily close the roads which led from Savoy along the Rhone; as for the Valtellina passes, since the time of Louis XII an agreement with the Swiss cantons, and in particular with the Grisons, had been maintained—and dearly paid for—which reserved the use of the passes to the King of France. Switzerland, moreover, was the country from which the best infantry was recruited. Holland also, Switzerland herself, and Venice were naturally interested in the closing of the passes to Spain. But Spain, for her part, barred the road to the south by fortresses.

Holland in those years was near to succumbing; Spinola's victory gave rise to thoughts of submission, of once more accepting the dominion of Spain. Henri IV became so disquieted that he sounded the States-General as to whether they would not prefer to accept him as their king. He supported them with money and troops, which in those days did not count as a breach of neutrality; and his skilful policy was so successful that on the conclusion of a twelve years' armistice Holland's independence was recognized by Spain; a result extremely galling to the Spanish Court—indeed, it was really for this reason that the proposal of a French marriage was rejected.

During the years of peace France had gathered strength; the wounds of the Huguenot war were healed; the nation was brave and warlike, although its army could not compare with that of Spain in organization, discipline, and endurance. And Sully was saving money; a war treasure and endless artillery material lay ready in the Arsenal.

Then, in the spring of 1609, arose the dispute concerning the Jülich-Clèves inheritance. Brandenburg, Pfalz-Neuburg, Pfalz-Zweibrücken, and Electoral Saxony all advanced claims to the duchies, and in France the Duc de Nevers and the Comte de La Marck did the same. The Emperor sequestrated the duchies, in order to decide the dispute as the feudal overlord. Henri IV, who had already taken part in the negotiations, complained of injury, and concluded an alliance with the German Protestants: but he found them inclined to caution. His interest in the matter was increased by a personal reason: the ageing monarch had fallen violently in love with Charlotte de Montmorency, the young wife of his cousin, the Prince de Condé. He had induced his favourite Bassompierre, for whom the old Connétable de Montmorency had destined his beautiful daughter, to renounce her, and had allowed the unpleasant Condé to woo her; as a husband he did not seem likely to be a dangerous rival; but he fled with his young wife to Brussels, and the Archduke Albrecht refused to surrender them. The king was beside himself. It is difficult to determine how far this passion and his personal exasperation caused him to feel less critical and restrained in respect of plans which he had doubtless had long in hand. At the time no one in his vicinity doubted that they were the principal motive of his action.

On the 17th of October, 1609, he had a long conversation in the gallery of Fontainebleau with the Maréchal de Lesdiguières, imparting to him all his views of the situation in the interior of the realm, the great nobles, the Huguenots, the necessity of absolute power in the hands of the king, the external situation, and the Spanish peril, and his intentions respecting Lorraine and Genoa. He certainly had similar conversations with others. Sully, later on, ascribed to him a "great plan" of dividing Europe after the overthrow of the Habsburgs, and founding a "League of Nations" after the pattern of the Greek Amphictyonic Council, from which only Russia was to be excluded; this League of Nations was to push back the Turks into the East, and Christian Europe would then enjoy permanent peace. It is improbable that the king, who was a realist in his political opinions, ever gave such a fantastic plan his serious consideration; but it is clear that he had considered and weighed the international situation, the possibilities which it offered him, and the necessities to which it constrained him.

Whatever the cause, he increased his armaments, although his expected allies shuddered at the thought of the perilous encounter, and most of them declared themselves neutral. Loans were raised and new taxes imposed which by themselves caused uneasiness in the country. But before his plans were realized, before the great war broke out between France and Spain, between Bourbon and Habsburg, the king was dead. A feeble-minded fanatic, who had heard that the king intended to fight "a war for the Protestants," stabbed him a few days before he was to enter the lists, as he was driving through a narrow street on the way to the Arsenal for a consultation with Sully, who was grand master of artillery as well as superintendent of finances.

The Dauphin, Louis XIII, was not yet nine years of age. The Duc d'Épernon, in command of the infantry, barred the streets leading to the Louvre immediately after the murder. No one knew what would happen next, and serious disorders were feared. The great nobles then present in Paris swore fealty to the king and queen; Marie de' Medici turned to the

Parlement; the *procureur-général* proposed to invest her with the regency. D'Épernon and other great nobles, who as peers had seats in the Parlement, urgently supported the proposal, and the queen was readily and unanimously proclaimed as regent. To the Court, however, this seemed a hazardous proceeding, and in order to mitigate it a *Lit de Justice* was held on the following day, in which the little king confirmed the decree.

There could be no further thought of the war; Jülich, indeed, was occupied and handed over to the Elector of Brandenburg and the Count Palatine of Neuburg; then the troops were demobilized. Difficulties were looming up at home.

All that Henri IV had won and accomplished came to naught. The political circumstances were not in any way different, but the disappearance of a notable leader, whose pre-eminence was admitted, released a host of repressed forces in the hearts of the ambitious and the covetous, who had hitherto practised restraint or observed discretion; and individual wills, being led by no common interest, united and controlled by no superior will, now took their own paths with disastrous effect. The psychical dynamic of the country was transformed.

The queen was a heavy, bulky person; sensual in an indolent fashion; limited, peevish, greedy of power, self-willed and yet pliable; "she always agrees with the last person who has spoken to her," wrote the Papal nuncio Ubaldini; "poor in words as in thought," said his successor, Bentivoglio; she wished to rule and yet was ruled. This woman now stood

MARIE DE' MEDICI
(Pourbus the Younger. *Ryks Museum, Amsterdam*)

helpless before the forces which suddenly surrounded her, threatening her from every side.

At first she retained in office her husband's old advisers. Sully, however, though she knew that he was of all the most capable, was, after a few months, thrust out of the ministry; he was arrogant and uncivil and much disliked; he disapproved of her Catholic sympathies for Spain and opposed the schemes of a Spanish marriage. The others were the esteemed and experienced Villeroy, who had been secretary of State for forty years; the president, Jeannin, Henri's most trusted confidant, an upright and honourable old gentleman, who took over the finances; and the chancellor, Sillery, a weak and timid individual: all three old men, inaccessible to new ideas, divided among themselves, and incapable of vigorous resolutions.

This being so, the attitude of the princes and the great nobles was one of doubt and hesitation. Condé had returned from Brussels; vicious, cold-hearted, avaricious, petty, and untruthful, unpleasing in appearance and intercourse, he was one of the most repulsive of men; but, as the nearest prince of the blood, he played the leading part; of his two uncles one, the Prince de Conti, was deaf and almost imbecile—he therefore did not count; but this could not be said of the Comte de Bourbon-Soissons, encouraged and influenced by his ambitious wife, Anne de Montafié. Even the lovely and talented wife of Conti, a daughter of that Duc de Guise who was murdered at Blois, found time, despite her many love affairs, to meddle in affairs of State. Then there was the Duc de Vendôme, a natural son of Henri IV and governor of Brittany;

the haughty Épernon, who as general of the infantry was in a position of authority, and, moreover, had the frontier fortress of Metz in his hands; the vain and garrulous Duc de Guise, the fidgety and fanciful Nevers; Henri de Rohan, the son-in-law of Sully, and his impetuous brother Soubise; and far away, in his stronghold of Sedan, which he possessed as a sovereign prince, the cleverest and most dangerous of them all—Henri Turenne, Duc de Bouillon, for ever plotting and planning; silent and reserved, a difficult man to see through; as a councillor greatly sought and seriously regarded by the nobles of the Court and others; a man with connections all over Protestant Europe; with influential relations in the German Empire as in France; spinning and laying his threads in all directions.

Each of these men thought only of himself; all were powerful, all had their vassals and adherents; all demanded fortresses, governorships, castles, estates, money and advancement; or else, like Bouillon and Condé, had various plans of their own. Soissons, as the eldest of the Royal princes—since Conti did not count—demanded the post of governor-general of the kingdom and the virtual regency; but this he did not obtain, for he died in November 1612.

Still in the background for the time being was another man who played a certain part at Court—a foreign body, soon to cause a dangerous ferment—the Italian, Concino Concini. A Tuscan noble, tall, pale, and handsome, he had come to Paris as a poor man in order to try his luck; he was master of the horse to the queen, and had married her lady-in-waiting, the daughter of her foster-mother—Leonora Dori, or Galigai, as she was called later, an ugly but astute and able woman with a sharp ferret-face, who was indispensable to the queen and had ruled her since her childhood. It was a typical lackey's intrigue that now began, and was to have atrocious consequences. The handsome, amiable Italian, with his great, mournful eyes, was always at hand, so that Henri IV was angered. But while the waiting-woman, affronted for her queen's sake, had made frantic and jealous scenes before the ever-amorous king, the master of the horse had contrived to intervene, and so had made himself acceptable also to the king. Both these people, and especially Leonora, who was infinitely avaricious, found a way to conjure ever fresh and ever greater gifts in money and estates and dignities from the queen, who had no will of her own where they were concerned; Concini became a great seigneur, Marquis d'Ancre, and one of the richest men in France; in a few years' time he possessed millions, and began to look about him for even greater positions and connections.

The great nobles were divided among themselves, and what with the intrigues, the secret alliances negotiated and entered into and dissolved again, the marriages purposely arranged only to be broken off, in all of which the Marquis d'Ancre was concerned, fresh dissensions were for ever occurring among the arrogant, conceited, and hot-blooded courtiers, and duels were fought which were very like murders. On such occasions they made a demonstration by riding out with hundreds of their adherents—the

Duc de Guise, on one occasion, with a thousand nobles—through the city; and one may imagine the clatter of hoofs and jingle of weapons in the narrow streets and squares of old Paris, and the commotion caused by such demonstrations!

No less menacing in the South were the powerful organizations of the Huguenots. The Huguenots had a hundred and fifty fortresses, for whose upkeep, after the Edict of Nantes, they received a yearly payment of a million livres from the State, which also paid their clergy; they were rich, for they had their adherents in the ranks of the nobles and the bourgeoisie; they were keen and industrious traders and great bankers, doubly hated because they were Protestants and because they had money. They could put thousands of nobles and thirty thousand war-bitten soldiers into the field; they had purposeful and ambitious leaders, like Bouillon and Rohan, or the hot-headed Soubise, who were beginning to thrust the old and famous and sober-minded Duplessis-Mornay into the shade; and even more dangerous were the fanatical preachers in their cities. They had their synods and, despite the Royal prohibition, a grand assembly, and were greatly excited when the secretly arranged Spanish marriage was announced, and at the same time a ten years' alliance with Spain was concluded. Louis XIII was betrothed to the Infanta, Doña Anna, while the heir to the Spanish crown, Don Felipe, was betrothed to the Princess Elizabeth of France. The Pope and the Courts of Europe had been consulted, and had unanimously given their assent to this work of peace. The Duc de Guise and the Catholic party were triumphant.

In the intrigues of the parties the queen favoured now this party, now that. The old ministers were all for tacking and compliance, lest the great nobles should take umbrage. And the nobles received fortresses and castles and governorships, and promotion for their adherents; the treasure saved by Sully was exhausted. But the recipients' appetite grew by eating; and also they began to be jealous of one another. And Concini, now a Marshal of France, though he had never fought a battle, was at last powerful enough to take a hand in the political game, and this inevitably led to fresh developments; for already the whole nation hated the enriched Italian with that embittered hatred of the foreigner of which the French are capable.

Condé, who had long ago taken offence because he had not been consulted in connection with the Spanish betrothals, and because he did not wield absolute authority, left the Court in February 1614 with a number of other gentlemen; and in those days such a proceeding was a sign of insubordination; for unless the great vassals had some particular mission to fulfil the sovereign preferred to keep them under his eyes. At the same time Condé published a mendacious manifesto, in which he deplored the critical state of the country, and, above all, lamented the squandering of the State's wealth—for which he himself was chiefly responsible; and he demanded that the States-General should be convoked.

While Villeroy and Jeannin at this juncture were in favour of vigorous action, the chancellor and Concini advised compliance, and the rebels were reconciled by further vast sums of money and concessions; the wedding festivities of the princes were postponed at Condé's request, and it was agreed to convoke the States-General. Nevertheless, the disorder continued. Vendôme remained in Brittany; his soldiery ravaged the land as though it were an enemy country; the Duc d'Épernon derided the Parlement, and Condé continually made fresh difficulties.

In the meantime the election of the States-General had been announced; letters were sent to the *baillis* and seneschals in the provinces, bidding them take care that only "honourable men, devoted to the king's service and inclined to peace and obedience," were to be elected. The Estates assembled in August 1614, amidst great festivities, and sat until March 1615. Great hopes were entertained of them, and were disappointed. Assemblies of this nature call for unusual tactical skill and experience, and these were completely lacking. The members were awkward and helpless; they spoke promiscuously and simultaneously and to no purpose. The three Estates were divided against themselves, and made contradictory demands, whereas nothing could have been accomplished save by united and purposeful procedure. The Third Estate demanded the abolition of the pensions, in the payment of which millions of the State's money flowered into the pockets of the nobles; the nobles, in reply, opposed the purchase and inheritance of office; the clergy wished the decisions of the Council of Trent to be sanctioned at last by the law of France; the Third Estate, being Gallican, violently opposed this suggestion, and demanded a "fundamental law" to the effect that "the King of France holds his power from God, and no spiritual or temporal power on earth can depose him "—a demand against which the clergy made a lively protest. Individual members like the scholarly and popular Cardinal Du Perron, or Robert Miron, the mayor of Paris, played a great part in the assembly without being able to advance matters; cliques were formed and dissolved; quarrels occurred, and even brawls between deputies, which gave cause for scandal; brilliant and forcible speeches were made; Savaron, one of the representatives of Auvergne, spoke movingly of the misery of the people; Miron, who was elected president of the Third Estate, distinguished himself by his energetic attitude, and nevertheless allowed himself to be won over by the Court; but on the whole the Third Estate were peculiarly unskilful, making loud and forcible requests and then giving way. When the nobles proposed that four representatives of the three Estates should be chosen by the latter from the *conseil privé* in order to examine the demands of the assembly, the Third Estate was opposed to forcing its advice upon the king. The Court wearied of the question. Meanwhile—on October 2, 1614—the king was declared of age, and confirmed in the Parlement the absolute powers of his mother. The courtiers wanted to have done; they gave the deputies ambiguous answers and arranged for a final session.

In this final session one of the two representatives of the clergy of Poitou, the Bishop of Luçon, Armand de Richelieu, who had already shown himself to be an able speaker in the negotiations between the deputies of the nobles and those of the clergy, was chosen to deliver the address to Their Majesties. He began with a reference to the custom of the Roman Saturnalia, which permitted the slaves at that season to say anything they pleased, to make any representations to their masters; here spoke free men, who yet by reason of their love were slaves; if then complaints were wrung from them by the excess of suffering, they would profit by the freedom which Their Majesties' benevolence allowed them. He spoke, blandly yet very plainly, of nuisances and abuses which were notorious, and of which one could and did speak more openly in the days of old, even before kings, than today; then, with a preacher's eloquence, he spoke of the blessings of a good and wise government; of the excesses of the Huguenots, which he deplored, and of the privileges of the clergy, which he wished to see secured; it would be a righteous and profitable thing were the higher clergy to sit on the privy council; and he concluded with Scriptural admonitions and expressions of homage to the king and queen. He was greatly applauded. In the existing state of affairs, and from the standpoint of the clergy whom he represented, it was a most adroit and tactful speech. To us it is significant as an event in the life of the orator; it had no political significance or consequences.

On the following day the deputies found the halls empty and the doors locked. They had been sitting in the convent of the Augustines; only the common assembly in the king's presence had been held in the great hall of the Petit Bourbon, where in later years

FRANÇOIS DU PLESSIS, SEIGNEUR DE RICHELIEU
(Sketch in sepia. Bibliothèque Nationale, Paris)

LEONORA DORI, MARQUISE D'ANCRE
(Pencil drawing by Dumonstier. Bibliothèque Nationale, Paris)

Molière had his theatre. They had been fooled; a few of them remained for a while in Paris, went daily to the convent, and followed the chancellor's carriage, or that of Jeannin, the Minister of Finances; at length the king sent for them and once more made reassuring declarations; and the last of them left Paris. The States-General were not again assembled until 1789. The Court made holiday with fêtes and ballets of great magnificence, in which the princes and princesses and the ladies and gentlemen of the Court appeared, and for which the celebrated Malherbe had written the lines.

A feeble government had won the victory over an even weaker opposition. The Paris Parlement went over to the opposition. By virtue of its own authority it did what had never been done before: it summoned the princes and dukes and the officers of the Crown to a plenary session, overriding a Royal prohibition, and in the "representations" which it addressed to the king it submitted its criticisms of the whole policy of the State, the new alliance, the foreign influences, and the extravagance of the financial administration. The Conseil d'État quashed the resolutions of the Parlement; the Parlement, protesting its loyalty and insisting on its rights, refused to submit; but this attitude was quite ineffectual.

Condé, who had demanded the convocation of the States-General, was the person most disappointed. Instead of adhering to him they had, as Rohan had foretold him, simply endeavoured to obtain a hearing from the king. As the Court now made ready to travel southwards in order to celebrate the long-deferred Spanish wedding, he declared that the rejoicings were once more premature; first, all the "abuses" should be abolished; he left Paris, however, with the Ducs de Bouillon, Longueville, Mayenne, and Nevers, and issued a new manifesto, in which he attacked the ultramontane policy of the queen and the " threat to the liberty of the conscience"; he raised troops, and entered into an alliance with the Huguenots. An assembly of the latter was prepared to take part in the insurrection; but not all the Huguenots were in agreement; a large proportion of them remained loyal to the Court; the Maréchal de Lesdiguières, one of the greatest seigneurs of France, who in his governorship of the Dauphiné was almost independent, and undertook military expeditions on his own account, placed six thousand men at the queen's disposal against the rebels, though he himself was a Protestant. Condé and his adherents were declared guilty of high treason; an army was sent against them, but no serious fighting occurred, though the troops robbed and plundered right and left. On November 21st the marriage of the young king took place at Bordeaux. The Infanta Anna, with a powerful escort to protect her from attack, had been brought from the Spanish frontier through the Protestant provinces. As soon as the marriage had taken place, first an armistice and then a peace was concluded, since the chancellor and Jeannin once more counselled submission; once more the insurgents were given millions, and Condé was appointed chief of the *conseil privé* as the best way of contenting him and rendering him innocuous.

Always distrustful and discontented, however, even after peace was concluded he did not return to the Court. Consequently the Bishop of Luçon, Richelieu, who in the meantime had become almoner to Queen Anne, and was already among the confidants of Concini and the regent, was sent to Condé, and persuaded him to return. In Paris the people greeted him with delight, for he was known to be the enemy of the Italian "favourite." The old ministers, with whom no one was contented, were dismissed, much to their indignation and dismay, and younger men were appointed in their place. The seals of State were confided to Du Vair instead of to the chancellor, who was irremovable, and Mangot became secretary of State; both were presidents of provincial Parlements. Claude Barbin, an unknown man of humble origin, once a small advocate in Melun, and now administrator of the queen's estate—a most able, energetic and honest man—was appointed Minister of Finances. These were all very different men from the feeble septuagenarians whom they replaced, but they were all devoted to Concini and were set in office through his influence. Leonora had not wasted the hours she spent with the queen. The new Ministry was thus divided; Condé, supported by the whole nation, seemed all-powerful, yet found himself overshadowed by the favourite, who enjoyed the confidence of the queen, and whose creatures sat in the highest places. The great nobles urged the prince to act and seize the actual power himself; but he, irresolute and wavering, ended under Bouillon's influence by conceiving a perilous plan; Concini, who was warned of it, left

Paris in fear of his life. Meanwhile his supporters took counsel; Barbin was apparently responsible for the energetic step that followed. When Condé, on September 1st, attended the *conseil privé* as its president, the courtyard and halls and stairs of the Louvre suddenly filled with armed men; there were bristling halberds on every hand; the prince was arrested, and at first guarded in the Louvre, and then transferred to the Bastille. Of the great nobles, some were submissive; others, and foremost among them the hot-headed Nevers, to whom Richelieu was dispatched in vain, proceeded to arm themselves; and Bouillon, who was quickest of all to take flight, remained inaccessible and impenetrable in Sedan.

Now the Maréchal d'Ancre, who promptly returned to Paris, was the master of France. Du Vair, who was numbered among Bouillon's friends and could not make terms with Barbin, was dismissed, and Mangot received the seals in his stead. Richelieu, who was to have gone to Spain as ambassador, was at Barbin's instance appointed secretary of State. The young Loménie de Brienne (who in those days still bore the name of La Ville aux Clercs) was obliged, as substitute for his father, who had long been secretary of State, to prepare the decree. Many years later, as an old man, he wrote in his memoirs: "I do not know whether it was my glory or my misfortune that I received this commission."

CHAPTER III

THE BISHOP OF LUÇON

The Bishop of Luçon came of a noble family of Poitou, which was by no means among the great families of France; he was what people called *un gentilhomme de bonne maison*. In this province of Poitou, which lay in the centre, between Northern and Southern France, and had fought with peculiar fury in the wars of religion, the Du Plessis—for that was their real name—had dwelt on the banks of the Creuse, in a poor, barren district, as the poor lieges of some vassal or other of the Bishops of Poitiers. A Guillaume du Plessis is mentioned about 1201, but it is only in the fourteenth century that the line of descent can be established with certainty. In the year 1490 François du Plessis inherited from his uncle, Louis de Clérembault, the domain of Richelieu, which lay many miles to the westward, near Chinon, in a more fertile country, and this devolved upon a younger line, which established its seat there and took its name from the fief. It was a rude, warlike breed that lived in the stronghold amidst the hills, filling its days with hunting, or the business of administering its fief, or feuds with its neighbours; or taking service in the king's armies. Louis du Plessis, the grandfather of the Cardinal, had four brothers, two of whom entered the Church; one of them, Jacques, became Bishop of Luçon. The eldest, François, attached himself to the Guises, distinguished himself under the terrible Maréchal de Montluc, and led his Catholic bands about the country until a bullet ended his career. A worse man still was his younger brother, known as Antoine, "the monk"; he was absolved of his vows by Cardinal Caraffa, and was one of the most dissolute troop-leaders and bloodhounds of the Guises. Terrible things were told of Antoine. Louis du Plessis, who seems to have been the most peaceable of the brood, married a Rochechouart. This marriage was apparently the most distinguished alliance that the family had yet formed; though the bride does not appear to have possessed much property. Louis was killed by one of his neighbours, a M. de Mausson, with whom he had a dispute. His son, François, lay in wait for his father's murderer amidst the osier-beds of a neighbouring stream, and struck him dead; he then fled to England. He is believed subsequently to have served in Germany and in Poland, where the Duc d'Anjou had been elected king. With him he found favour, and when the duke, as Henri III, ascended the French throne, he returned to France with him and was appointed Grand Provost—that is, the chief police-magistrate of the Court, whose jurisdiction included the king's castles, and, when the Court was outside Paris, all the territory within a radius of ten miles. In this capacity he had to perform duties of historical importance; it was he who, at Blois, after the murder of the Duc de Guise, arrested the most prominent of his adherents of the Third Estate; and he captured the Dominican Jacques Clément, the murderer of Henri III. He was, therefore, one of the first to swear allegiance to Henri IV, and was by him confirmed in his office. He is described as a pale-faced man with a stern and gloomy expression; he had little learning, but was clear-headed and sagacious. Under what conditions the ruined nobles were then living we may judge from the fact that when he died, in 1590, at the age of forty-two, his family, although he had held an important post, and possessed the domains of Richelieu, Nueil, Neufville, Vervolière, Mausson, Chillou, and Coussay, were obliged to pledge his decorations in order to meet the cost of his funeral. The possession of a fief meant lordship, not administration; the barony of Richelieu was administered by the truant, Philippe Messeau de La Girardière, who, in addition to fulfilling certain formalities and obligations, paid for it a yearly rent of fifteen groats.

François de Richelieu married Suzanne de La Porte, who came of a good bourgeois family; her father, François de La Porte, was a celebrated jurist, and the president of the advocates' guild in Poitiers. He left three sons and two daughters. Henri, the eldest, who was ten years old when his father died, inherited the barony, in accordance with feudal law, "as far as the capon flies"; otherwise his inheritance consisted mostly of debts. He went early to Court, and Henri IV gave him a pension of 9,000 livres. To the second son, who entered the priesthood, he gave benefices. The family possessed a sort of reversionary interest in the episcopal throne of the neighbouring diocese of Luçon, which was almost always given to a Richelieu; until Alphonse was old enough an administrator was appointed, and the episcopal throne remained unoccupied. The youngest of the boys, Armand Jean, was born in Paris, on May 9, 1585, apparently in the Rue des Boulangers, and his mother nearly died at his birth; the record of his baptism may still be seen in the books of the commune of St. Eustache. Two marshals of France, Armand Gontauld, Duc de Biron, who came to so tragic an end, and Jehan d'Aumont, and his grandmother, Françoise de Rochechouart, were his sponsors.

So long as mother and children could remember they had lived in fear and anxiety. Huguenots and Catholics fought one another all over the province; again and again their brutalized bands rode through the district and committed the usual atrocities; again and again the inhabitants were forced to defend themselves or flee into the town; pestilence, too, was no stranger; death, terror, and destruction were everywhere. Even in the year 1593 the neighbouring fief of Faye la Vineuse was plundered and burned by a band of Huguenots, who committed all imaginable atrocities; and then came the Duc de Mercœur with his Catholic troops, who behaved no whit better; at last, in order to secure some protection, the local nobles formed a volunteer *gendarmerie*.

The boy Armand was delicate and often ill; his mother, when she speaks of him in her letters, calls him *mon pauvre malade*. He was not yet ten years old when he once more came to Paris; to the Collège de Navarre, which had been the school of his father and his uncles, and of the kings Henri III and Henri IV.

LOUIS XIII AS A BOY
(Pourbus the Younger. *Uffizi, Florence*)

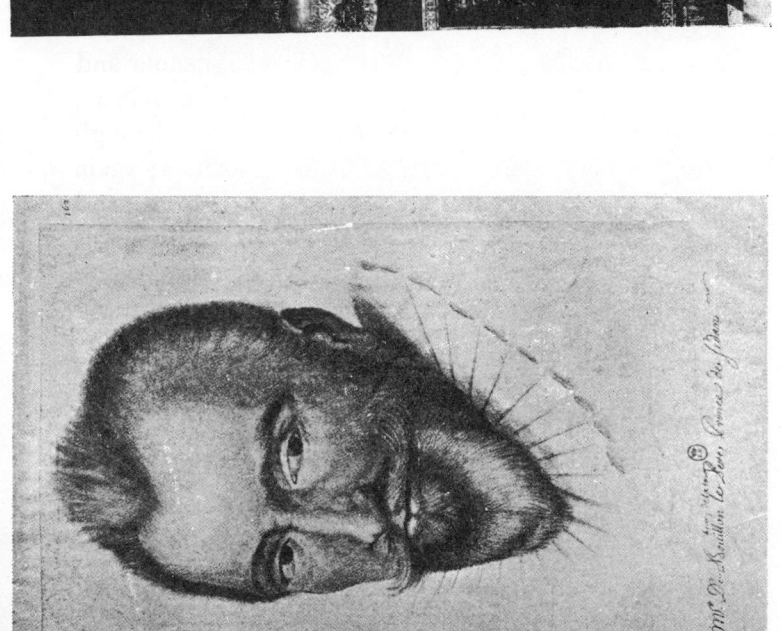

THE DUC DE BOUILLON
(*Drawing in red chalk by Dumonstier. Bibliothèque Nationale, Paris*)

THE BISHOP OF LUÇON

At that time he bore the title of Marquis de Chillou —derived, in accordance with the usage of the day, from one of the fiefs of his family. He is said to have been a very diligent and ambitious scholar, and was noted for a remarkable memory. He then went to the academy of Monsieur de Pluvinel, where young nobles learned to ride and fence; they were likewise instructed in heraldry, and learned something of mathematics and of military history; but above all they learned assurance, and elegant, courtly manners. Armand, though delicate and ailing, was intended for a military career. But his elder brother, Alphonse, who was always a little eccentric, suddenly declared that he would not become a bishop; he would not be a secular priest at all; no, he must be a monk, and he entered the Order of Carthusians. The bishopric had to be kept in the family, so Armand was obliged to take orders. Accordingly he studied theology, and was now known not as the Marquis de Chillou, but as the Abbé de Richelieu. While he was still at the university and had scarcely attained his majority, and long before he had reached the canonical age, he was created the titular Bishop of Luçon. After the concordat concluded under Francis I the sovereign appointed the prelates in France, and Henri IV was well disposed to the Richelieu family. Armand's elder brother, the Marquis de Richelieu, was a great favourite at Court; witty and elegant, he was one of the "seventeen seigneurs" who set the tone; his brother-in-law, the Baron René du Pont-Courlay, who in 1603 had married the eldest sister, Françoise, was chamberlain and captain of the guard. To these circumstances, as well as to the youthful abbé's talents, his exceptionally early nomination may be ascribed. The king applied to the Pope for a dispensation in respect of the age-limit, and Richelieu journeyed to Rome, where Paul V—a Borghese pope—was reigning; he was presented to the pontiff, who was favourably impressed, and at Easter 1607, though only in his twenty-first year, he was consecrated bishop by the Cardinal de Givry. Brilliantly intellectual and learned, he was launched upon a brilliant career. On returning to Paris he passed his theological examination as bishop, and on October 31st, again against all the rules, he was received into the Collegium of the Sorbonne. In the following year Cardinal du Perron, the Grand Almoner of France, appointed him to preach the Easter sermon at Court. In the winter of 1608, whether inspired by extreme shrewdness and calculation or out of regard for his health—for he was again frequently ill—or because he lacked money, or for other reasons, he retired to the provinces and his see of Luçon, which he entered shortly before Christmas. It was "the most miserable, the filthiest, and poorest bishopric of France"; "I am a beggar—we are all beggars here," he wrote to a lady of his acquaintance in Paris. In the little town, which was more like a village, he devoted himself wholly to his duties. He chose the priests of his diocese with care, and kept a watch upon their conduct; he settled disputes among the nobles, and busied himself with ecclesiastical affairs. Many evenings were given to study in the dismal rooms of the episcopal "palace," lit only by candles, or dimly burning lamps and troublesome fires, of whose smoke he complains. There he wrote a catechism, *L'Instruction du Chrétien*, which had a great success, and was translated into several languages, and a treatise "on the manner in which the Protestants might be converted to the true faith," and other theological works. He made acquaintances in the district—for example, the Abbé Duvergier de Hauranne, the grand vicar of the warlike Bishop of Poitiers, Châteignier de la Rocheposay; and he had a good friend in the dean of his own chapter, the Abbé de la Cochère, of the Bouthillier family—one of the bourgeois families of the district, which was allied and attached to his own. And at this time, also, he became acquainted with a fanatical and visionary monk, the Capucin Père Joseph—otherwise François Le Clerc du Tremblay, of a family of official standing in Anjou. All these were to play a more or less important part in his life.

He was an exemplary bishop and an admirable administrator of his diocese, it being his nature to proceed, in all sorts of business, logically and energetically, and in the manner of a ruler; and this, not by virtue of his spiritual vocation, but by reason of his innate political talents. It was important that he should win friends and reputation in his own estate. In 1610 he hoped to be elected as deputy to the assembly of the French clergy in Paris; but he was disappointed. Throughout his life he retained the habit, in all matters of especial importance, of setting forth logically in writing, for himself and others, the exact position of affairs and the right lines to follow; so in the same year he wrote his "Instructions and

Principles which I have laid down for myself respecting Behaviour at Court." "To speak as little as possible, to be silent often, to withdraw adroitly, without lying, when the truth is dangerous, to burn all letters received, to be modest in coming forward; I have not held myself in sufficiently when I have spoken with great lords; not to appear distracted when others are speaking; the King likes quick and frank answers and loves to be praised; to cease speaking when the King drinks; everything depends on his favour." He had no idea of burying himself in the provinces: all his thoughts were centred on Paris, where he might win that "favour" on which every career depended—Paris, where his brother was already making his way. He was in constant communication with this brother, and with others in the capital; he was exchanging letters with various ladies of the Court who were well disposed towards him; the queen's maid of honour, Selvaggia Vincenti, wrote to him that he ought really to return to Paris quickly; she often spoke of him to the queen. To return was his dearest wish, and when he suffered his first severe disappointment, when Henri IV, the patron of his family, was murdered, he wrote a letter to the queen, his widow, in which he assured her of his unshakable loyalty and his deepest devotion; but his more experienced brother did not deliver the letter; he himself anticipated no advantage from this conspicuous excess of zeal.

The five-and-twenty-year-old prelate, devoured by ambition and restless scheming, grew despondent in the unsatisfying and hopeless remoteness of his province; impatiently he resolved to go yearly to

THE BISHOP OF LUÇON

Court, in order that he should not be forgotten; but after the very first visit he returned disappointed and dispirited; his glowing hopes had not been fulfilled; and he had even not possessed the means to make an adequate appearance. "It is a very bitter thing to be a poor nobleman," he wrote at the time. But he continued to exchange letters with the king's confessor, the Jesuit father Cotton, and with the influential Père Bérulle, the founder of the congregation of the Oratorians, who was intimate with the queen, and with various members of the higher clergy; he also sent letters full of devotion—letters of condolence or congratulation—to such powerful personages as the Duc d'Épernon; and one letter "with profoundest respect" to Sully, the once so powerful but then fallen minister, who at that time was governor of Poitou, with a request for some favour; in later years their relations were curiously reversed. By the end of 1613 he was again in Paris. This visit was certainly important; he must have sounded certain prominent persons in the vicinity of the regent; it seems that the Bouthilliers had introduced him to Barbin, and that Barbin presented him to the Maréchal d'Ancre. On February 12, 1614, soon after his return, he wrote the Italian a letter from Luçon, in which he assured him of his loyalty and his readiness to serve him, just as the great nobles were gathering head against him. Relatives and friends were working for Richelieu in Paris and the provinces, and six months later he was elected to the States-General. His election he owed principally to the Bishop of Poitiers. He had reason to be satisfied with the success of his début in the assembly; he had played a part there. But as yet he foresaw no immediate results, no advantage to himself; once more he left Paris and withdrew to his diocese. There another of his colleagues, the Bishop of Bayonne, Bertrand d'Eschaux, a benevolent prelate, older than himself, profited by a chance opportunity to obtain him a post as almoner to the young Queen Anne, the wife of Louis XIII. Another candidate was within a hairbreadth of being nominated before him; as yet he was none too sure of his footing, and was already distrusted as a place-hunter. But at all events he had an office at Court, even though he had as yet no opportunity to exercise it. What steps he then took, what threads he spun, we do not precisely know; the times were uneasy, and the Court was continually moving from place to place; it may have been for these reasons that he was not immediately summoned, or his always unreliable health may have been responsible; for in a letter written in April 1616 he excuses himself to the queen-mother for not having presented himself at Court; an attack of fever was responsible. However this may be, in the spring of that year he finally migrated to Paris. He had there a house in the Rue des Mauvaises Paroles, a street that has long ago disappeared; it was not far from the old Bureau des Postes, and ran from the Rue des Bourdonnais to the Rue des Lavandières, very nearly where the Rue de Rivoli lies to-day. His career was now determined. He was made a *conseiller d'État*, and as such drew an income of 2,000 livres yearly; he was appointed also private secretary to the queen, a post which yielded him an additional 6,000 livres.

Then followed his two missions to Condé in Berry and to Nevers in Champagne; and lastly he was appointed secretary of State, with a stipend of 17,000 livres. Immediately after receiving this appointment he learned that his mother was dead. She died on November 14th, in her sixty-first year, in the old Richelieu manor where she had spent so many years of distress and difficulty, of anxiety for the fate of her children and the continuance of the house. Only his sister Nicole had been with her. Richelieu's brother, the Marquis, wrote to say that they must postpone the funeral until the bishop could accompany him. Richelieu was an affectionate son and brother; his love for his family was perhaps the warmest emotion ever known to this cold and calculating man. But already the most difficult affairs of State were pressing upon him so urgently that he was compelled "in bitter affliction" to abandon the journey, and his mother, after three weeks' delay, was buried without him in the village church of Braye, where the bones of the Cardinal's ancestors lay, until, in the French Revolution, the vault was broken open and destroyed. All his life long Richelieu had to pay for his splendid career at the cost of his humanity.

Half a century earlier the secretary of State had been merely a scribe and forwarding-clerk for the king's affairs of State, waiting on his liege's commands with a portable inkstand slung at his side. Only since 1559 had be borne this high-sounding title, and for some time longer, at the sessions of the *conseil privé*, he sat at a side-table, performing the duties of a clerk. But his post, in the natural course of events, was constantly becoming more important and influential, and was beginning to approximate to that of the modern minister. Barbin, who thought very highly of Richelieu, and was the most prominent and energetic man in the new ministry, entrusted him with the important departments of war and foreign affairs, and gave him the precedence among the secretaries, which greatly annoyed the touchy Brienne. Richelieu was by birth the most aristocratic member of this ministry, which consisted otherwise of gentlemen of the robe or men of still humbler origin. This fact, and the support which he received from the higher clergy of the country, gave his personality additional importance. He was thin, pale, and slender, with a small, pointed beard, such as even the clergy wore in those days; he was always elegant, and every inch a noble, and, as a general thing, he did not wear the robes of his profession. An abbé who had some dealings with the cabinet council of those days describes very vividly how he used to see the youthful bishop and secretary of State sitting at the back of the chamber, dressed in black and leaning comfortably back in his chair. One can almost hear him speak—coolly, with a smiling, superior affability in the small, bearded face—and note in his bearing the assurance and resolution of a young man of rank who has a very great opinion of himself.

In those years he was possessed by ambition for ambition's sake; by the desire to play a leading part, rather than by any definite plan; in order to achieve a career he had entered into the policy of those whose side he had taken and who had given him advancement—the Spanish-Catholic policy of the queen and the Maréchal d'Ancre. The Spanish ambassador, the Duke of Monteleone, reported to his Government after Richelieu's appointment: "The Bishop of Luçon is my intimate friend; no one could be more devoted to God and our Crown." On the other hand, the two envoys of the Venetian Republic, Ottavio Bon and Vincenzo Gussoni, wrote to the Signoria: "The appointment cannot be regarded as favourable to Your Excellencies; he was intended for the Madrid ambassadorship, belongs to the Spanish party, is always in the Spanish Embassy, and is said to be paid by Spain." The new nuncio, Guido Bentivoglio, wrote to the Holy Father: "To the cause of religion, the appointment of a prelate so eminent for his learning, his eloquence, his conduct, and his religious zeal can only be favourable."

At first there were insurrections and civil war at home. The Duc de Nevers, one of the most restless and extravagant of men, who was most of all embittered because his plan of a great crusade against the Turks had not been taken seriously by the Court, continued his warlike activities. He wished to be Emperor of the Levant. Bouillon, whom Richelieu called "the demon of rebellion," the man with the unfathomable eyes and the crafty mouth, stood behind him and egged him on; he had been forced—so he said—to flee from Paris without his shoes; but the pair of silk stockings which he spoiled thereby would cost the French Court many hundred pairs of boots. He was scheming to win Protestant Europe and those princes who were related to him for the French rebels, since France, thanks to the mercenary Italians who were ruling there, had fallen into line with Spain, and the Protestant interests in Europe were in danger. After years of maladministration and disorder the French Court had neither troops nor leaders nor money. Barbin, who was an able financier, was the first once more to bring forward a regular budget; fresh taxes were imposed, mercenaries were hired from Holland and Switzerland, and the Comte d'Auvergne, the natural son of Charles IX, who was reputed to be an able general, but had been imprisoned during the reign of Henri IV, was released from prison and placed at the head of an army, while two other bodies of troops were fitted out under the command of the Duc de Guise and the Maréchal de Montigny. Richelieu's energy manifested itself in these quickly-taken measures, and also in an unusually severe proclamation against the rebels. "This time," he wrote, "the affair will not end in a treaty!" And when the Duc de Nevers, in alarm, attempted to open negotiations through his sister, the Duchesse de Longueville, and the Papal nuncio, he coldly refused to parley. As a matter of fact, the Royal armies were quickly victorious over the insurgents.

In her foreign policy France had assumed a position entirely opposed to the policy pursued by Henri IV. Richelieu found himself in a net, and was seeking to extricate himself by the extremest subtlety. He was confronted by the old problem of French policy, the more so in that complications were once again developing in Italy. In Mantua and Montferrat, bordering on Savoy, the house of Gonzaga was regnant, and the

Gonzagas had repeatedly intermarried with the house of Savoy. Since the death of the Duke Francis, in the year 1612, the hunchback Duke Charles Emmanuel of Savoy, one of the most crafty, energetic, and ruthless politicians of the time, had laid claim to the inheritance of Montferrat. He was in alliance with England and with Venice, and had issued a manifesto to all Italians, in which he summoned them to unite with the house of Savoy against the oppressive power of Spain.

Venice was at war with the Archduke Ferdinand; the new viceroy of Milan, Don Pedro de Toledo, was threatening both the republic and the duke of Savoy. Once more the Alpine passes, as the roads of communication for the armies, were of the greatest importance.

When Richelieu took over the department of foreign affairs he dispatched a circular letter to the ambassadors of France abroad, in which he assured them of his co-operation, and at the same time asked them for their advice, and, above all, for exhaustive reports, and yet rather bluntly reserved his own decision. The ambassadors, who were older than Richelieu, and persons of some consequence and of long experience in their calling, were by no means pleased by the youth and the decisive tone of their new chief, and, after the manner of officials, they pointed to the errors of procedure of which he was guilty, and in other ways endeavoured to make difficulties. Richelieu promptly determined to replace them by new men. For the time being he sent trusted and qualified emissaries on special missions to the Protestant powers, in order to counteract the dangerous influence of Bouillon, and also to explain the attitude of France. To Germany he sent M. de Schomberg, who was himself of German descent, being the son of a German colonel, Kaspar von Schomberg, who in the time of Henri III had supplied that monarch with cavalry raised in the Empire. Richelieu praised his "German loyalty"; for a brief interval Schomberg went over to the Catholic opposition, but apart from this period Richelieu made use of him all his life as a reliable assistant, valuing him greatly and promoting him. Schomberg was to make it clear to the Protestant princes that so far from France being bound to Spain, it was rather Spain that was bound to France, and that in Paris, now as formerly, the friendship of the Protestant princes was greatly valued. Efforts had been made to obtain the hand of the Prince of Wales for a French princess, and France was supporting Holland, Savoy, and Geneva. . . . In a Royal dispatch to the French ambassador at the Emperor's Court (M. de Baugy), it was stated that the aim of Schomberg's mission was merely "the welfare of the realm"; but he had, as a matter of fact, yet another mission: to intercede for the future election of the Archduke Ferdinand as King of Hungary and Bohemia; these countries must not be allowed to fall into the hands of a Spanish Habsburg; and at the same time France would be making herself agreeable to Austria. The whole venture was characteristic of Richelieu's initiative and intellectual independence; indeed, the mere fact that France had once more a policy was significant, for the old ministers who had preceded

THE BISHOP OF LUÇON

Richelieu, whether out of timidity or indolence, had invariably followed the path of least resistance. Yet he was bound and hampered. At that time the Spanish ambassador was admitted to the sessions of the *conseil privé* in Paris. The Court, the clergy, and that part of the nation which had adopted the views of the League were in favour of the Spanish alliance; the great nobles were against it because Concini was in favour of it; the Protestants opposed it vigorously, and a great part of the French nation, whether Catholic or not—the people who called themselves "good Frenchmen"—were likewise hostile to Spain and in favour of the old policy of Henri IV. Profiting by these tendencies, Richelieu hoped, out of the infinite complexity of the situation, to win for France a sort of mean position—the position of a mediating power. The French Court was to be arbitrator in the threatening conflict of the Powers.

Meanwhile matters ran their course; the Duke of Savoy was already seriously threatened by the Spanish armies; whereupon the Maréchal des Lesdiguières, the "King of Dauphiné," marched into Savoy on his own account, with 7,000 foot and 500 horse, and effected a rescue. Richelieu was obliged to repudiate the Maréchal, but the tone of his repudiation was not very peremptory, and he addressed the Maréchal himself with the greatest courtesy, perhaps because he was afraid that the self-willed old man might attach himself to Bouillon and incite his co-religionists to rebellion.

Meanwhile the Venetian envoys requested that France should permit the Grisons, which since the time of Louis XII had been allied to France, and was pledged to open or close the passes only by agreement with France, to conclude an alliance with Venice also, and to open the passes to the Republic. The queen received them in Richelieu's presence, and consented to everything; but the young minister soon realized, or was made to realize, that he had been too precipitate; that the disposal of the passes would have meant a defiance of Spain for which he dared not be responsible; he was obliged to retreat, to put off the importunate envoys with evasions. Disappointed and incensed, the envoys contrived to ruin the French minister's plans, and their own into the bargain; all the Powers repudiated the court of arbitration which Richelieu had proposed; it was discussed only in Madrid and in Rome. He welcomed the peace which was concluded, but he had suffered an absolute defeat. Even the special missions had yielded little result. Like other men in a similar case, he felt that those about him were rejoicing in his defeat. The French ambassadors were not sorry to see their haughty young chief humiliated; even the nuncio made no secret of his delight. Richelieu angrily recalled the ambassadors in Rome and Venice.

This did not greatly help him. But he was one of those men who blunder once only; and no one knows how he would have proceeded had not the tragic happenings in France completely altered the aspect of affairs.

CHAPTER IV

THE DEATH OF CONCINI

RICHELIEU had found the queen in power as regent, with Concini as her favourite; he had therefore attached himself to them. The government in which he was secretary of State was a government by grace of Concini; the ministers were the servants of the queen, and in effect of Concini.

Since he had been declared of age in the autumn of 1615, Louis XIII was by law the ruler of France, and sooner or later must be ruler in actual fact. He was a healthy, frolicsome boy, though wilful and imperious, and prone to terrible fits of rage. He had been strictly brought up and frequently punished. His mother was harsh and severe to him. He stammered and was intellectually backward, but was thoroughly imbued with a sense of his dignity and importance. When the Duc de Vendôme, after his insurrection, came to the Court at Nantes in token of submission, the king addressed him as follows, trembling with rage: "In future serve me better! Remember that it is your highest honour to be my brother!" Although he was delicate, he was tenacious and inured to fatigue; he was greatly interested in all military matters, and was constantly hunting; he was particularly fond of shooting, and if the weather was bad he indulged in the sport indoors, firing at birds which were released in the *salons* of the château.

Otherwise he still amused himself with childish games, nibbled marzipan, and had all sorts of hobbies. There was little in him of his jovial father, excepting his courage; he had nothing of Henri's sang-froid.

The queen, greatly enjoying her position as the ruler of France, intended to retain it as long as possible. The sixteen-year-old king was permitted to meet no one who might turn his thoughts to serious things; he was allowed only to play and hunt. In games and hunting he passed his days; he heard Mass, and paid brief visits to his mother and his young wife, with whom he did not as yet cohabit. If he concerned himself with other matters his mother rebuked him. Leonora spoke of him as "an idiot." Some while previously he had been given a chamberlain who had been page to various gentlemen of the Court, and finally to Louis himself, and who had a special understanding of the king's favourite sport. He was not far off his fortieth year, but looked younger than his age; he came of a family of petty provincial nobles. He was Charles Albert de Luynes; he took his name from a fief so small "that a hare could spring over it." He had two brothers: one called himself De Brantes, after a small vineyard which he had inherited, and the other De Cadenet, from a little island in the Rhone, which was covered when the stream was high. All three now served the king. They were said to have been so poor that at first they had only one court suit between them, which they wore in turn; but they were all handsome men; even the eldest, with his curling hair, his large, gentle eyes, and his ingratiating voice. There was something quiet and indeterminate and friendly about him. The king found in him a pleasant playmate, and became passionately attached to him. He called for him in his sleep, and when for this reason his governor, the Maréchal de Souvré, wished to remove the man, he fretted himself into a fever. Marie de' Medici thought it better to reward and promote the insignificant young man on whom her son was so dependent, in order to get him on her side. He was made castellan of the Louvre, and was given other small and profitable appointments.

While the king and his chamberlain hunted or played or whispered together in the king's apartments or the park, the stout, indolent queen sat upstairs in her own rooms with her swarthy foster-sister and waiting-woman, now Maréchale and Marquise d'Ancre, who of late had been ill and irritable, and when she was out of temper made scenes with the queen herself. Beside them was the pale, handsome Italian with the nervously restless eyes, "the Marshal," as he was called, the man who counted. He, too, was ill; he suffered from a severe double rupture. Then there was the elegant young bishop and secretary of State, always welcome to the ladies, who recognized his ability without suspecting its colossal magnitude; the young bishop who, with smiling devotion, paid court to the queen. How far their mutual interest extended we cannot say; probably the queen felt a half maternal and half womanly inclination for the young prelate. The Galigai, on the other hand, often complained that she "could not bear those eyes"; they gazed at her too keenly. She was in constant dread of being bewitched, and was growing more and more eccentric. She had about her not only her chamberlains and nobles, but persons of lesser account; intriguing Italian priests, Jewish physicians and astrologers, and all sorts of strange individuals who wandered in and out of the Court.

The Maréchal d'Ancre held the reins, even though the queen was sometimes angered by his frequently absurd pretensions; she was accustomed to give way to him and his wife, and Richelieu, during this period, wrote him some very meek and obsequious letters. The Italian felt that he was standing on uncertain ground; that all France hated him, from the highest to the lowest. After the arrest of the Prince de Condé —who was still confined to the Bastille—his palace was plundered and destroyed by the infuriated populace. He was no coward, but neither was he a thinker; he was vain, restless, melancholy, and suspicious; no statesman but a mere adventurer; and he was guilty, as Richelieu subsequently stated in his memoirs, of the greatest stupidity that can be committed by a man who has recently come into power; instead of behaving as unobtrusively as possible he made the greatest possible display of his power. He was a foreign body in the country which he ruled; he ruled it, not because he had any ideas in his head, but simply because he had the power to rule it, which power he owed to the illegitimate influence of a servant. He would gladly have married some woman of noble birth; he had thoughts of Vendôme's daughter. His marriage had been a mere intrigue; and he and his wife hated one another, though held together by necessity, so that there were often furious scenes between them, and they even came to blows. The future he often regarded with dread. When he lost his dearly loved daughter, early in 1617, and Bassompierre called to condole with him, he wept sorely and said in his bad French: "Signor, I am lost; Signor, I am ruined; Signor, I am miserable!" He said, moreover, that he could foresee his undoing through the wilfulness of his wife, and he told Bassompierre how he had risen in the world; how poor he had been once, when his father, the chancellor of Tuscany, had fallen out of favour; how many millions he possessed now, and how he wished he could leave the country.

He had often such fits of depression, but on recovery he was presumptuous and insolent as before, keeping ambassadors waiting in his ante-room and treating the ministers like lackeys. "By God, Monsieur," he writes to Barbin, "I have reason to complain of you! You have induced the queen to write to me in such a fashion. . . . What the devil do you think of me, you and the queen?" His anger is so great it "eats his bones." It even makes him insolent to the king; he sits in his presence when a deputy of the Parlement is being received; he neglects to uncover his head, refuses him the money he asks for, and makes merry over his games.

It was plain that he lost his nerve. He feared for his life; he felt that he was an alien; he armed himself and concentrated troops. He now wanted to become an independent prince; he wanted, for his greater security, to be granted the fortress of Amiens.

The young king began to be angry, with a morose and restrained anger; and his confidant was Luynes. It would have been a singular thing if Luynes had not thought of his future; if he had not told himself that now, while he was in such favour with the prince, who must soon be the ruler of all France, was the moment for action; he must strike while the iron was hot. Who knows what these two discussed in those long days and nights? The young king was not very intelligent; he was even less experienced, and very easy to influence. The queen grew afraid once more, and so did the Maréchal. "Alberti, Alberti, my friend," he said one day to Luynes, impetuously clasping his hands, "the king has looked at me with angry eyes, *con occhi furiosi*; you must account to me for that, Alberti; I hold you responsible!"

The queen had some time before this informed the king that she was now anxious to place the government in his hands; and he had refused to accept it, as she had hoped and expected; looking all the while at Luynes, who stood by, with his gentle, handsome face, discreetly silent.

Even the ministers grew alarmed; they would play the game no longer. Richelieu spoke to the nuncio, telling him that he was tired of politics; asking him whether there was no prospect of ecclesiastical promotion for him, an archbishopric or a cardinal's hat? His desires were never petty. He and Barbin approached the queen and explained that the Maréchal's humour, and his policies, made further co-

THE DEATH OF CONCINI

operation impossible; and they suspected, or rather knew, that Concini, who now trusted no one, was anxious to get rid of them. The queen promised to let them know her decision in a week's time. Richelieu, with the cunning of the serpent, sent his brother-in-law, the Baron de Pont-Courlay, to Luynes, offering the king his services and his secret reports of the ministry's proceedings. In the perilous atmosphere of the Court, where all the walls had ears, and treachery threatened from every side, a man must seek for protection in all directions. One can imagine how the wholly and half-initiated, and those who only felt or suspected that danger was in the air, were for ever anxiously whispering in the shadowy halls and corridors of the Louvre, which were full of so many bloody memories of treachery and murder.

The catastrophe occurred before the queen could inform Richelieu of her decision; even before he could himself draw clear of the affair.

A strange conspiracy was concocted in the Louvre; a conspiracy of the supreme head of the State and his sorry household against the Government. Luynes and his brothers were themselves of no importance; and under them served even pettier nobles, some of them men of unsavoury reputation. These men, and a secretary of Barbin's, Guichard Déagent by name, with some servants and under-gardeners, took counsel together. The matter went on for weeks, and the secret was still kept. Luynes's ambitious hopes, it would seem, were not unmixed with fear, and apparently he not only put it to the king that he was, after all, the sovereign, and had merely to exert his will; but he also inspired him with a deadly fear of evil intentions on the part of the marshal and the queen. Various plans were considered; Luynes, who was timid by nature, was for fleeing the Court; Déagent, the shrewdest and most energetic of the conspirators, was for arresting or murdering the marshal. But for such a purpose men of sterner mettle were needed. One of the captains of the guard, Baron de Vitry, who had grown up at Court, and whom Henri IV had always addressed by his Christian name of Nicholas, was asked by a huntsman whether he was willing to do the king a service. Vitry, as the Cardinal de Retz recorded afterwards, a man of small intelligence but absolutely fearless, declared that he was ready. He was given the commission of arresting the Maréchal d'Ancre. The arrest was to have been made in two days' time, on a Sunday, but time and opportunity did not suit, and it had to be postponed until the following day.

On Monday, April 24, 1617, saddled horses stood ready in the courtyard of the old fortress-like Louvre; Vitry had posted reliable men in the rooms and corridors; he himself sat on a chest in the guard-room of the Swiss, dangling his legs and waiting. Just as the Marshal entered the courtyard, about ten o'clock in the morning, Vitry went out and approached him, but was held up by someone or other, and lost sight of the Italian; but he asked after his whereabouts, and found him reading a letter, surrounded by an obsequious crowd. Vitry pushed his way through to Concini, laid his hand on his arm, and declared that

THE DEATH OF CONCINI

he had orders from the king to arrest him. "*A me!*" cried Concini, and clapped his hand to his sword. "Yes, you!" answered the captain, and signed to his men, who drew their pistols and shot him down. Vitry had obtained full authority to kill the man if he offered resistance, was certain that he would resist, and wished him to do so, for once dead he could not return to power and take vengeance. Scarcely a hand was raised in defence of the murdered man; only the captain of his guard, a M. de St. Georges, had drawn his sword. Subsequently Richelieu took him into his service. In the excitement and confusion that ensued, a Corsican, Colonel d'Ornano, who was in the secret, lifted up the young king and showed him through the window to the soldiers and nobles in the courtyard. "Thanks! Many thanks to you!" he cried out of the window, and they cheered him. A waiting-woman of the queen's, who had heard the shots, called out to Vitry from an upper window, asking him what had happened? Vitry composedly told her; she closed the window and ran to the queen. "Woe's me!" cried the queen. "I have reigned for seven years, but now I can expect a crown only from Heaven!" Someone asked her whether they should tell the Maréchale what had happened. "Tell her! Sing it if you like! I have other things to think about!" replied the bewildered woman. "I don't wish to hear any more of the people! I warned them often enough! Why didn't they go back to Italy?"

After some time she sent her master-of-horse to the king, who sent a message to the effect that he would treat her as his mother, but henceforth he himself would be the ruler. Presently guards appeared before the door. She was a prisoner.

The Galigai learned the news soon enough. Even she cried: "My husband was a fool! I told him what would happen!" She wept and scolded. Then she hid all her jewels and money under her mattress and went to bed. But Vitry's guards forced their way into her room and bade her get up; they searched the room, removed all her valuables, and took her away to prison; she had not even time to draw on her stockings.

Richelieu was in the Sorbonne, with one of the rectors, when he heard of what had been done. He would not have believed it of Luynes. He at once went to the queen, who was then in the Louvre, where his presence was desired. In one of the halls the young king was standing on a billiard-table; Luynes had made him climb on to it so that all might see him. There was a great throng of people about him, cheering him. Weeping with joy, he had told the advocate-general, Servin: "Now I am really king!" When he saw Richelieu he cried angrily: "Now I am free of your tyranny, M. de Luçon! See that you take yourself off!" But Luynes interposed, praising the bishop, who had always given sensible advice. His two colleagues, Mangot and Barbin, were already arrested; he was protected by his clerical robes; against him it was not so easy to proceed; moreover, he had had certain dealings with Luynes. He heard that the old ministers would be recalled, and attempted, as though it were a matter of course, to take part in their deliberations; but Villeroy

THE CONNÉTABLE DE LUYNES
(Pencil drawing. Bibliothèque Nationale, Paris)

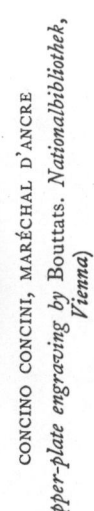

CONCINO CONCINI, MARÉCHAL D'ANCRE
(Copper-plate engraving by Bouttats. Nationalbibliothek, Vienna)

THE DEATH OF CONCINI

went up to him and asked him drily in what capacity he was there. Richelieu did not answer. No one spoke to him or paid any attention to him, and as soon as he could do so unobserved he disappeared.

He drove off to the nuncio. On the Pont Neuf he ran into a howling, cheering mob; the populace had dragged the Italian's corpse out of the courtyard of the Louvre, where it lay covered with a cloth, into the street. Raving men and women had wreaked their rage upon the dead; the body was horribly torn and mutilated. The bishop's coachman was about to order the crowd roughly to make way for his master, but Richelieu, who realized the danger of recognition by the populace, rebuked the coachman severely, crying; "These are honest folk, who would die for their king! *Vive le roi!*" and won through unmolested. On the way back he preferred to make a wide circuit.

In his memoirs, which were compiled and revised by many different hands, but under his supervision, so that he was certainly responsible for individual passages, and for most of the statements, it is recorded that Luynes offered him a place in the Government, which he did not accept. This is not very probable, and no one else mentions the incident. In conversation with the nuncio he alluded suggestively to the post of envoy to Rome, but the nuncio replied that the new rulers would presumably employ their own people. He remained in the service of the queen, the only counsellor left to her, and undertook her negotiations with the Court. It was decided that she must go to

Blois and there remain. It was more than a week before she was permitted to leave her room to take leave of her son. What she and the king said at this interview was settled and written down beforehand. When the king entered Luynes and his brothers preceded him, and he did not let go of Luynes's hand; Bassompierre and the Prince de Joinville followed him. The queen, who began to weep, held her handkerchief and her fan before her face; she then led the king to the window. She said, as had been agreed, that she regretted that the realm had not been administered to his satisfaction; she had expended the greatest pains on its administration. The king expressed his thanks and assured her that he would treat her with filial affection. Now she was supposed to kiss him; but she begged him, as a favour, that Barbin might be released and restored to her. The king looked at her without replying; she repeated many times, urgently, that this was her only and perhaps her last request. But the king was silent. "Well, then!" she said, and gave him her farewell kiss. He bowed and went. She kissed the young Prince Gaston passionately, and then urgently made the same request of Luynes; but the king cried repeatedly: "Luynes! Luynes!" and Luynes left her. Now she leaned against the wall and wept bitterly, so that she scarcely noticed those who bade her farewell. Her carriage stood waiting; she stepped in, and the procession moved off. Overhead the king stepped out on the balcony to watch her departure, and he even ran through the corridors in order to gaze after her carriage as it drove across the Pont

THE DEATH OF CONCINI

Neuf, always with the same cold and reserved curiosity. In the city some regarded the procession with compassion; others shouted angry words of abuse. In the last carriage sat a fallen minister, the Bishop of Luçon.

CHAPTER V

LUYNES

THE first thing the new men did was to divide the spoils. On the very day of the murder Vitry was made a marshal of France. Luynes was created a duke and a peer of France, and he married the daughter of the Duc de Montbazon, Marie de Rohan, a lively, restless, sensual creature, exceedingly pretty, with blue eyes and auburn hair. He was passionately in love with her; and she was destined to play a great part. His brothers, too, made brilliant marriages; one was created Duc de Chaulnes, and the other Duc de Luxembourg; all three received governorships and other dignities. Relatives, friends, and supporters thronged about them. The great insurgent nobles, rejoicing in the downfall of their enemy, returned to the Court; only the Duc d'Épernon was too haughty and overbearing readily to accept a man like Luynes, and the Duc de Bouillon also held aloof. "Only the sign is altered; the inn is still the same," he said.

Proceedings were initiated against the dead marshal; a letter of Richelieu's, in which he thanked him for his appointment, was adduced as proof that the murdered man had arrogated to himself the kingly power. His widow was accused of sorcery, condemned to death, and executed; she bore herself better in misfortune than in success. The problem was retrospectively to justify the violent deed that had been committed and to confiscate the property of the murdered man. A few lesser people were likewise condemned, and some of them executed; and all Concini's servants were expelled from the capital. The Jews were the victims of violent hatred, and were likewise banished, because Concini had Jewish physicians and astrologers about him. The proceedings against Barbin were the most protracted. He, as always, behaved in a firm and manly fashion, refusing to speak against the queen or his friends, despite the traps which were set for him. Luynes feared no one so much as this talented and energetic man, and did his utmost to secure a death sentence; but the French judges were true to their reputation; the majority could neither be corrupted nor intimidated; they found Barbin guiltless, and condemned him to banishment in order to save him from worse things.

Meanwhile the queen remained in Blois, in obstinate melancholy, broken by outbursts of rage. A little court surrounded her, but she was closely observed, and was made to feel her downfall and her impotence. Richelieu was her counsellor. He felt the whole difficulty of his position. He wrote the most submissive letters to Luynes, and even to lesser people, such as Déagent, who was now controller-general of finances, and for a while possessed great influence. But he could not win their confidence. Insignificant men were conscious of his intellect and his power, and feared him accordingly; he was conscious of their fear, and knew that he stood on dangerous and unstable ground. While he was still considering and waiting on events, he received a letter from his brother, who had been warned by the

Marquis de Châteauneuf, who had come from the council chamber, that the banishment of the bishop was imminent. All was lost, and he would do better to withdraw of his own free will; whereupon he took leave of the queen for a week in order to visit his diocese.

It had been a false alarm; but while he was in Luçon he received a letter from the king, praising him ironically for his wise action, and instructing him not to leave the town without orders. The queen was beside herself at the thought of losing her sagacious counsellor, whose presence was so acceptable to her, and she wrote both to him and to the Court despairing letters of entreaty, which were all unavailing.

Once again Richelieu had to vegetate wretchedly in the provinces. He had made a mistake in attaching himself to those who, however powerful, had no firm roots in the soil of France; the bland, insignificant Luynes had been shrewder in cleaving to the one securely established power—that of the king.

Once again he busied himself in ecclesiastical affairs, and since four Protestant preachers had presented to the king a memorial upon a sermon which the king's new confessor, the Jesuit father Arnoux, had preached before the Court against heresy, he wrote in answer a memorial upon the four principal points of the Catholic faith, which he submitted for approval and had printed. The noteworthy point about this memorial, which, like all that he wrote, was logical and temperate yet sharply controversial, is that it analysed the political insecurity of Protestantism, which implied innumerable rebellions of the Protestant subjects against their sovereign, and above all the danger to an authority based on tradition inherent in any religion which was founded on independent criticism. At the same time, however, he declared that it was madness to employ violence in matters of faith; the Protestants must be converted, but only by patience and kindness and the force of example.

This memorial had a great success, and this success further prejudiced his position. As before, he was regarded with distrust. In vain he wrote to Luynes, and to all manner of other people: to Père Joseph and Cardinal Borghese, begging them to make his peace with the Court. When the queen turned to him for counsel, Luynes gave his approval, but when a number of letters had been exchanged he laid them before the king, in order to prove how dangerous the bishop was; and Richelieu, his brother, and his brother-in-law were banished to Avignon.

The county of Venaissin, in which Avignon lay, was a Papal enclave in Provence. In the sunny southern city on the Rhone, with its cliff-like ramparts, its fortress-like palace, and its many churches and convents, inhabited principally by immigrant Italian families, priests and religious, and Jews, Richelieu spent the most melancholy period of his life. He had rented a house near the Minorites' convent. There, in the first rebellion and despondency of exile, and also, perhaps, as a precaution against whatever might befall, he wrote a defence of his conduct, the *Caput apolo-*

geticum. With all the trenchant and logical eloquence at his command, he showed that he had done nothing that others who stood in favour had not done, and that his conduct in becoming a minister, and in all that he did as a minister, was upright and perfectly in order. Then once again he busied himself with his books and his theological studies, mixing almost exclusively with ecclesiastics, although he knew that among them he was under constant observation. Failure and banishment were followed by grievous misfortune. The Richelieus had arrived in Avignon in April 1618 : in October they received the news that the young wife of the Marquis de Richelieu, Margeurite Guyot des Charmeaux, who had remained at Richelieu during her pregnancy, had died in childbed; the son whom she bore died a few weeks later. The Marquis and his brother-in-law were given leave to go home, and Richelieu was left alone in Avignon. Ill and hopeless, on February 8th he made his will, which has been preserved. In it he provided substantially for the church of Luçon and the seminary which he had founded there, and expressed the hope that the chapter would be vouchsafed a bishop who would remain in Luçon, and, abjuring all worldly things, would live only to serve God.

While he was meditating on his end in such profound despondency, suddenly, on March 7th, a mounted messenger arrived from Paris: M. de Le Clerc du Tremblay, the brother of his friend, Père Joseph, bringing him a letter in the king's handwriting, by which he was recalled to favour, and instructed with all possible speed to join the queen-mother at Angoulême, in order to resume his old position as her counsellor.

On the very next day, in bitterly cold weather, he took his seat in the stage-coach and rode northwards over the snow-covered roads. He had been just eleven months in Avignon. Shortly before reaching Lyons he was arrested by order of the governor, who thought thereby to do the Government a service. He had to apologize profoundly when M. du Tremblay arrived and produced the king's letter. Near Limoges he was on the point of being arrested again, by some troopers of M. de Schomberg's, who was expecting some very different travellers. On March 27th, which was Easter Wednesday, he arrived in Angoulême, and was joyfully received by Queen Marie; and there he learned from his friend, the Abbé de la Cochère, what had happened. The queen, who could not reconcile herself to her fall from power, and could think of nothing but returning to Paris, had in Blois been kept under increasingly strict observation, and her freedom had been progressively restricted. More than anything she felt the disrespect which was shown her. The envoy of her father, the Grand Duke of Tuscany—a Signor Bartolini—had been expelled from France because he had visited her; and Colonel d'Ornano, who had been sent to her with a message, had dared coarsely to threaten her. Almost all those whom she trusted had been dismissed; many had left of their own accord; her circle of acquaintances and her servants were almost all in Luynes's pay; her walks were restricted, and she heard, or perhaps feared, that she was in danger of being even more strictly confined. Meanwhile those who dreaded her return were seeking to secure themselves against it, and through the agency of Père Arnoux, the king's confessor, a document was laid before her, according to which she was to swear "by God and the angels" to comply with all the king's commands. Fearing lest worse might befall her, she signed it. But in her mind she was seeking a means of escaping from her wretched position. Among the persons surrounding her was a Florentine, an Abbate Rucellai, a witty and talented but eccentric and ill-tempered man, who had already played a certain part in Rome, at the Papal Court, and later in Paris. He kept open house, had an admirable cook, and was witty and entertaining, and a gifted musician, though splenetic and peculiar: for example, he lived in deadly fear of every change of weather and every draught. But he could forget all his fears and all his love of luxury when he had anything of importance in hand. At the queen's command he went to Sedan, to the Duc de Bouillon, the wise man of whom all sought counsel. His advice was that the queen should appeal to the Duc d'Épernon.

When Bouillon said that nothing was greatly altered he had summed up the situation and the actors. Luynes was an indigenous Concini; perhaps less cultivated; conscious in the depths of his mind of his insignificance, and for that reason all the more fearful and distrustful. He had none of the qualities of a statesman, and was devoid of political ideas. Uncertain and inexperienced, he had little influence in the privy council; political measures were always decided on by the old ministers; but he had power over the king, and in personal matters especially he had to be consulted. He, however, was chiefly concerned to retain his position and to enrich his family. Before long he was hardly less hated than his predecessor had been, although he still enjoyed the favour of the king, whose nature it was to submit to an alien will and to cling to those to whom he was accustomed to submit. The feeling of all the great nobles was once more hostile to him; the Duc d'Épernon felt peculiarly affronted; his untameable pride and arrogance made it difficult for anyone to get on with him, and now, half in disgrace, he was sulking in his fortress of Metz. Rucellai possessed a benefice not far from Metz, and to this he now repaired, but even he was treated with the greatest arrogance and insulted by the duke. The duke, for his part, had been highly discontented with the queen's treatment of him during her regency. Nevertheless, Rucellai ventured to send to Metz another Italian, a confidant of his—Vincenzo Ludovici, the former secretary of the Maréchal d'Ancre. He alighted at a tavern and asked a confidant of the duke, Du Plessis by name, who was an absolute stranger to him, to beg permission for him to visit the duke. Ludovici had brought a letter from the queen.

The astonishing adventure that followed is described in all its details by Girard, the private secretary and biographer of the Duc d'Épernon. How the duke immediately guessed that the matter in hand must be a perilous one; how he sent an intelligent servant to the tavern, who embraced the stranger and asked after persons whom he invented on the spur of the moment—

for even Metz was full of spies; how the duke cautiously declared himself to be ready under certain conditions; how ciphers were agreed upon and secret messengers sent to and fro; how Rucellai took up his quarters for months in the Hochstein, where the duke was living, and thanks to the confidential servant was even fed out of the ducal kitchen. His chance acquaintances supposed that he had some pretty woman or other hidden away in the Hochstein.

The negotiations lasted from July to January. Often they escaped detection only by a miracle. Once a page of Rucellai's, having scented a dangerous secret, went to Paris instead of to Blois, in order to sell it to the Court, but he was not at once admitted to Luynes, and happened to hit on a councillor of the Parlement who was an adherent of the queen's, and he—professing to act on Luynes instructions—paid the page for his documents and sent them unopened to Blois.

In the meantime Épernon had repeatedly asked the Court for leave to visit his governorships of Angoumois and Saintonge, but could not obtain it. Day after day his horses were bridled and saddled, taken out through the gates, and brought back in the evening, in order to keep them exercised, until the whole city was used to the sight of them. In January, on a mild, sunny day, he broke out with "only" a hundred gentlemen and guards, all armed, and fifteen loaded pack-mules; his son, the Marquis de La Valette, who remained in Metz as commandant, kept the gates of the city closed for three days, while a whole company of carabiniers rode along the roads leading to Paris and barred them, so that no news of the duke's escape should reach the

Court. Nevertheless, the news of the duke's evasion reached Paris in the course of time; the Court sent messengers to him, who ran into the arms of his men and were sent on a false track. Mounted troops were sent after him, but missed him. The nearer his flight came to succeeding, the greater the danger, for Épernon was to join the queen in Loches, which was only a day's journey from Blois, but it was also only a day's ride from Paris.

The night before these events Du Plessis had secretly entered the château, and was joined upstairs by the queen's young master of horse, the Comte de Brenne. On the following night two of her guards joined them. Her confidential waiting-woman, an Italian, had packed her coffer, her jewels, and the necessary clothing, and Brenne had made fast a rope-ladder outside the window. The guards and her waiting-woman were begging her not to risk the uncertainty of the fate that awaited her without . . . when there came a rap on the window, and Cadillac, Du Plessis' servant, leapt into the room, threw himself at the queen's feet, and announced that the duke had entered Loches. He himself had ridden from Metz in five hours—he had started at eight, and it was then one o'clock—and had climbed straight up the ladder. In the darkness they climbed out of the window, high up in the castle wall, and down the rope-ladder to the platform, by which time the queen, a ponderous woman, was so terrified that she refused to climb down from the rampart to the road, preferring to slide down a steep escarpment, sitting on a cloak. In the road she was met by two of her officials, but when they saw the half-veiled woman among the men they suspected quite a different sort of adventure, which greatly amused the queen. At the last moment they were unable to find the carriage—it was waiting in the dark in a side-street—but finally they drove off, and half-way to their destination met Épernon's troopers. A few days later, on March 1, 1619, they entered Angoulême, where the duke had mustered some five thousand foot and eight hundred horse for the queen's protection.

As early as February 25th she had written to the king, from Loches, a letter justifying her action; the late king had advised her in any difficulty always to apply to Épernon. The Court was greatly perturbed. The courtiers were aware of the feeling in the country; the queen would once more be powerful; a great party would rise in support of her; they foresaw a civil war and the greatest danger to the State. Épernon was deprived by decree of all his dignities. The old president, Jeannin, advised against open war. Only one man was known to the Court who was cleverer than all the rest and had influence over the queen—Richelieu. Père Joseph and the Abbé de la Cochère had proposed his recall. To him, accordingly, the Court appealed; it was for him to bring the situation under control. He came, to the great disappointment and indignation of Rucellai and all those who were advising the queen. They all warned her against him. The whole political genius and tactical mastery of the man appeared in his very first step. To the astonishment of the others he declined to take part in their deliberations. Then they became anxious for his criticism and pressed him for his opinion. Being questioned, he replied that he would do the contrary of what had hitherto been done, and recommended a dignified but conciliatory attitude towards the Court as the only possible solution. Rucellai and all the lesser people now threatened to leave the queen; even the Duc d'Épernon sent word to him that he would do better to return to his diocese, for here he had too many enemies. He had no thought of doing so. For Rucellai, who had really risked his head and had performed great services, this was a tragedy. He was furious, and finally went over to the Court. Richelieu's superior sagacity and his personal influence over Marie de' Medici were decisive. The civil war which had already begun—for Schomberg's cavalry were already before Metz—was averted, and on May 12th the treaty of Angoulême was concluded, in which the queen was granted a governorship, fortresses, a Royal establishment, and the free choice of her advisers. It was realized that this was Richelieu's work, and he was regarded with renewed consideration; his quick recovery after his downfall provided matter for reflection. He himself knew well what he had achieved, and saw as his next aim the cardinal's hat, which would give him princely rank.

As the first token of his gratitude and favour the queen appointed his brother, the Marquis de Richelieu, governor of Angers. This exasperated the Marquis de Thémines, who had himself hoped for the post, and he made certain remarks about favourites. A duel resulted, in which Henri de Richelieu fell. His death was the heaviest sorrow Richelieu had ever known; he loved his brother, and saw in him the founder of the great family for which, in his pride as a noble, he longed. The hopes of his line were destroyed. After this disaster he was one of the bitterest enemies of duelling, and in later years, as a minister, he punished it with ruthless severity and sought to uproot the practice.

The whole country, ever conscious of the patriarchal position of the sovereign house, demanded a visible reconciliation between mother and son. For this reason Luynes was anxious for them to meet. Richelieu likewise seemed to wish for the meeting, yet he hesitated. Luynes was lavish of ambiguous promises. However, when at last, after six months of mutual bargaining, the principals met first at Gonzières and then at Tours, it was not Richelieu but Épernon's son, the Archbishop of Toulouse, who was proposed for the cardinal's hat. "There existed no greater liar than M. de Luynes," we read in Richelieu's memoirs: "his lips made every sort of promise, which he was resolved never to keep." He himself lied to Luynes no less freely, as to everyone whom he wished to win over or deceive; but he was alone in his exceptional ability. Sensitive as he was, moreover, and greatly as he suffered under every defeat, he always had himself under control. Where another, angered by the nomination of a rival, would have complained and set to work to oppose it, the sagacious Richelieu interceded for the Archbishop of Toulouse.

The meeting of the king and the queen-mother was unsatisfactory. It could not have been otherwise. They both wept, and did not know what to say to one

HENRI II, PRINCE DE CONDÉ
(*Copper-plate engraving by* Huret. *Nationalbibliothek, Vienna*)

another. The weather was hot and oppressive. Marie de' Medici saw the hated faces of those who had overthrown her, and asked unpleasant questions of Luynes and Vitry. She saw a handsome young queen in her place; she saw that her day was over. Scarcely had the two parted when fresh mutual discontents arose, fresh causes of discord, which time only aggravated. An endless exchange of diplomatic notes ensued, the gist of which was expressed by Richelieu as follows: "Luynes entreated the queen to come to Court and feared nothing so much as that she might come; the queen declared that she wished to come to Court and had no thought of doing so." Richelieu was assured that it was his business to undertake and carry through this affair of the Court; he could do it if he wished; and nothing was too great for him to demand if he would do it. Richelieu remained impenetrable. Time worked for the queen, who was constantly growing more powerful, since Luynes was for ever making fresh enemies, who then went over to her side. Already they were making proposals for a change in the mode of government. Once again a number of the great nobles left the Court, though not indeed the best of them; the very youthful Comte de Soissons, with his ambitious mother; the incapable Longueville; the cunning but faint-hearted Vendôme. They, after all, had provinces of their own, and the more valiant Épernon and Mayenne were on the queen's side. On the other hand, Condé, who had been released from imprisonment, was now all for the Court. Richelieu at this period played a very impenetrable part. He avowed that he was against any armed resistance or aggression on the part of the queen's adherents, for he did not believe it would be successful. It would seem as though he was playing his own game, and playing it with infinite shrewdness; he warned his party against the blunder of taking up arms, yet he was not sorry to see them commit it. The step was taken—and to Richelieu's advantage.

On paper, according to the calculations of M. de Marillac, the queen's power was very considerable. But as soon as the king seriously opened hostilities the house of cards collapsed, for all the provinces welcomed him with rejoicing and all the fortresses opened their gates to him. Bassompierre led the king's army against the bridge-head of Ponts-de-Cé, an island that lay in the Loire between two fortified bridges, which was the key position between Northern and Southern France. Up to the last moment negotiations were continued, but in vain. On August 7, 1620, the king's troops attacked, and almost all the nobles who were fighting for the queen lost their heads and decamped. "You see a man who wishes he were dead!" cried the Duc de Vendôme, as he rushed into the queen's chamber. "You need only have remained on the battlefield!" retorted one of her maids of honour. The action was known as "the farce of Ponts-de-Cé."

Richelieu, who had foretold all that happened, but had perhaps done nothing to hinder it, was again sent to the king's camp as the last helper in extremity. He read the secret of the timid Luynes: the constable, who was, above all things, afraid of his own helpers, and especially of Condé, was ready for anything.

Coolly and cautiously, Richelieu obtained the most favourable conditions for his mistress. She had only to promise to live at peace with the Court. All her adherents were pardoned. Richelieu was now assured in writing of the cardinal's hat, and as a closer bond Luynes offered him the hand of his nephew, M. de Combalet, for Richelieu's niece, the daughter of M. de Pont-Courlay.

Twice Luynes and the Court had violently overthrown the party to which Richelieu belonged, and on both occasions it had been forced to appeal to him, and by him had been defeated in negotiation. Never has the power of the intellect won such a manifest triumph over arms.

CHAPTER VI

THE OLD POLICY

This was the time when the hundred years' war of religion, which in France had raged most violently in the sixteenth century, but whose most destructive explosion was still to occur in Germany, was once again rekindled. This recrudescence involved some extraordinary developments in domestic and foreign politics.

The Huguenots in France were fanatical and restless, hated and distrustful. Now an old cause of contention reappeared. When Henri IV went over to Rome he was compelled to promise to return the stolen Church property in Béarn to the bishops and the convents. In the year 1617 the bishops, in the assembly of the French clergy, had alluded to this promise, which for twenty years had remained unfulfilled. Louis XIII wished to fulfil the promise; the nobility and bourgeoisie of Béarn refused to do so; and the Huguenots all over France were aroused.

This meant difficulties for France. And at this time the stability of Austria seemed to be threatened. The Palatine minister, Count Dohna, had already prophesied its dissolution when the old Kaiser Matthias died; and this prophecy seemed likely to be fulfilled. From the north Vienna was threatened by the Bohemians, under Thurn, and from the south by Gabor Bethlen and his

THE OLD POLICY

allies the Turks. Protestantism, having conquered the north of Europe, seemed to be forcing its way far into the south. The Bohemians had elected as their king the young "reformed" Elector Palatine, Friedrich, the son-in-law of the king of England. When this plan was submitted to the most highly regarded of Protestant statesmen, the Duc de Bouillon, in Sedan, through whose hands all threads appeared to run, he had expressed himself very cautiously and ambiguously in respect of the "good young prince," but would do nothing to hinder its execution. On every hand—in Flanders, Holland, Bavaria, Spain, Italy, and Venice —men were taking up arms on one side or the other.

The decision hung on the attitude of France. In October 1619 Ferdinand, who on August 8th had been elected Roman Emperor, sent an envoy extraordinary to Paris—Count Wratislaw Fürstenberg, who was to intercede with the Catholic king for the threatened Catholic interest. Bouillon was the spokeman of the Protestant cause. Louis XIII was pious; after Luynes, of the men who surrounded him the clergy had the greatest influence over him. Luynes, too, was pious, and always turned a willing ear to the nuncio. The Spanish envoy, the Duke of Monteleone, had regained his former influential position. Condé had become a zealous Catholic. Nevers was preaching his crusade against the Turks. In the whole of France there was perceptible a striking renewal and intensification of Catholic feeling under the influence of the Jesuits, the Capucins, the newly founded or newly imported order of the Oratorians, and the Carmelite nuns. Of the ministers, the chancellor, the old Brûlart de Sillery, was all for the Catholics; but his son, De Puyzieux, who since Villeroy's death had been secretary of State for foreign affairs, was a man who never took sides decisively, so that in any event he might be in the right. Old Jeannin once alluded to the terrible power of the House of Habsburg, but thought that now, when Austria was weak and threatened, one should help her for the sake of "the religion." On Christmas Eve Père Arnoux preached on the dangerous menace of heresy. This sermon seems to have had a decisive effect on the mood of the king. He promised the Kaiser assistance, and first of all sent an embassy to Germany, which was, if possible, to negotiate a peace. It consisted of the Duc d'Angoulême, the Comte de Béthune, who had just returned from Rome, the brothers Sully, and the Abbé de Châteauneuf.

But then the quarrel with the queen had held up everything else. So soon as the reconciliation was effected the king marched into Béarn, restored Catholic worship there, returned their property to the clergy, and established a Parlement in Pau.

While the events and decisions of domestic politics were thus following their course, the old personal quarrels and difficulties in the Court, in respect of the influence of personalities at the Court and in the Government, were continuing as usual. Richelieu must at this period have spent most of his time in the Luxembourg. Marie de' Medici had had the palace built by Jacques de Brosse; it was to remind her of her native Pitti. It was commenced in 1615, two years before her fall, and completed in 1620. There she worked with the bishop, who was expecting his elevation to the cardinalate. The Abbé de la Cochère had already been sent to Rome to prepare the way for his nomination; but Luynes and the secretary of State, Puyzieux, assured the nuncio that the proposal was not intended seriously. "The man is crazy and my enemy," said Luynes; "I have no such intention"— and Bentivoglio reported the words. Soon after this the queen visited the nuncio and begged him to expedite the affair. He told this to the secretary of State, and they both laughed. Richelieu himself visited the nuncio in order to assure him of his devotion to the Holy See. Bentivoglio, of course, understood what was meant, and replied with vague civilities. He could not endure Richelieu, and wrote to Rome that the insane ambition of this man must be humbled. Richelieu felt that the affair was at a standstill, that there must be opposition somewhere, and he was even warned that this was the case. He applied to Luynes, who assured him that the thing was as good as done; he would die before he would break his promise. The favourite would have preferred that Rome should refuse the nomination; but Richelieu was in favour at the Papal Court, and the nuncio would not lend himself to the other's game. He demanded a definite declaration. "If he is appointed, good; if he is not appointed, still better!" said Luynes. Then, on the 2nd of January, 1621, the Archbishop of Toulouse was created cardinal, but not Richelieu, although two hats were available for French cardinals.

The queen, who during this period often felt herself to be affronted, was now furious. Richelieu was silent; those around him were vociferous. The people of France were growing more and more discontented with Luynes and with the policy for which—with a certain justification—they held him responsible.

The French embassy to Vienna had congratulated the Kaiser on his election, and had reassured him: France did not recognize the Elector as King of Bohemia. But in order to defeat him the Kaiser needed the help of Bavaria and the League, which were opposed by the forces of the Union of the evangelical princes. Negotiations took place in Ulm. The envoys went thither and arranged, as they were commanded, a favourable peace between the German States, which did not, however, include Bohemia. Maximilian of Bavaria was able to go to the Kaiser's assistance undisturbed, and on the White Hill, on the 8th of November, 1620, the Winter King was disastrously defeated, while Spinola invaded the Palatinate from Flanders, and the new governor of Milan, the Duca de Feria, took possession of the Valtellina passes. Austria and Spain had recovered their terrible power. France had made herself unimportant and powerless; the French envoys had played a ridiculous part; they felt this themselves, and wrote disconsolate dispatches; the Catholic policy of the French Government had re-established the world-power of Charles V. Bassompierre was sent to Spain as envoy extraordinary, in order to obtain at least the evacuation of the passes; and on the 13th of April, 1621, he signed the Treaty of Madrid, by which Spain promised the evacuation in terms that were not quite definite, and of whose fulfilment he himself had no expectation. In the meanwhile the Protestants of France had held a new general assembly in La Rochelle, which, in defiance of the Royal prohibition, contrived to deliberate until May, divided France into eight districts, and raised and equipped an army. The leaders were fanatical preachers; it was a sort of religious demagogy. The Protestant magnates, Lesdiguières, Bouillon, and others, drew back, as a great number of the Huguenots, and in particular many of the nobles, were during all these movements loyal supporters of the king, and even fought under his colours against their rebellious co-religionists. The two Rohans and the Marquis de La Force were at the head of the movement. Once more a Royal army marched southwards. Luynes, who on the 2nd of April was created Constable, although he had never been a soldier, and always feared and avoided any fighting, was nominally at its head. Louis XIII, thanks apparently to his father's influence in his childhood, was, with all his piety, an enemy to intolerance; he was fighting only the political opposition to his commands. Those who surrounded him were mostly, of course, of a different way of thinking. Bassompierre and De Pontis, in their memoirs, have given a vivid description of this bloody war of siege, which ravaged the south of France. Many strongholds were captured; and the curious admixture of barbarism and knightliness which was characteristic of the period found expression in the alternation of frightful atrocities and honourable clemency and humanity in these hostilities, which finally came to a standstill before Montauban, which remained impregnable.

But many "good Frenchmen" took no part in the civil war, while the European hegemony of France crumbled to nothing. It fairly rained pamphlets against Luynes and the policy of the Court, such as the "Christian Truths for His Most Christian Majesty," the "Advice of dying France to her King," the "Chronicle of the Favourites," and the rhyming "Complaint of the Constable's Sword," which was never permitted to leave the scabbard; for Luynes was no warrior. Forerunners of the modern journalist entered the field: the Canon de Fancan, the Abbé de Morgues, remarkable men in whose character, life, and activities, as in those of so many political agents, there was something secret and inexplicable. These men were now on an intimate footing with Richelieu; later, when they became dangerous, he coldly and inexorably removed them from his path.

His influence, always opposed by those who were powerful at Court, was none the less constantly increasing; chiefly through the agency of his ecclesiastical friends. Many of them had long believed in him unreservedly, and had worked for him as the one hope of the Church; and foremost among these were Père Joseph and Cardinal Du Perron; the impetuous Père Arnoux, the king's confessor, already called him "the future head of the Government"—and for that he was soon afterwards dismissed from his post; so much Luynes could accomplish, for the king was still subject to him, although even he was beginning to weary of him. Luynes' new dignities had so far gone to his head that, like Concini, he had lost all sense of proportion and equilibrium. "Here comes the king!" said Louis one day to Bassompierre, standing at the window, as Luynes, followed by the whole Court, passed by beneath. "Never fear," he said on another occasion, "I shall make him spew up what he has swallowed!" But he was still afraid of his own creatures, and always had some secret or other, now with this and now with that seigneur at Court; and they were never allowed to tell anyone if the king confided anything to them, or showed them any favour.

Then suddenly Luynes died, on the 3rd of December, 1621, of erysipelas, which he had contracted in the camp before Montauban, in which all sorts of diseases were raging. Louis XIII took the death of the man to whom he had once been so passionately attached coldly enough, and turned at once to his mother. She had once more retired from the Court in anger, to pay a visit to her friend and adviser at his château of Richelieu, and she now sent him to the king in order to express her condolences. But by the time of Luynes' death the former ministers were already in office; old Sillery, feeble, but greedy of gold and power, and his son Puyzieux, the "State hermaphrodite"; and the king had not the experience, nor as yet the resolution, to make any fundamental change. The fanatical and insignificant, though always serious and sedate, Cardinal de Retz had for a long while—though possessing no real influence—been president of the *conseil privé*. All feared the queen, and even more they feared Richelieu, whom they knew to be at her back; with the fear which in all times and places has leagued mediocrity against genius. When

RICHELIEU

Retz died in the autumn of 1622, the pious, amiable, and impolitic Cardinal de La Rochefoucauld was made president, in order to keep out the man they dreaded. The ministers sought an ally in the Prince de Condé. The queen might, indeed, enjoy her son's "confidence," but she should not possess a voice in the council. "They feared that she might bring me in," says Richelieu in his memoirs; "they knew that I had some judgment, and they feared my intellect." Like Mirabeau in a similar situation, he proudly suggested that they might, as far as he was concerned, declare him permanently excluded from the Government. But such a proceeding was too open and wholesale for the jealousy of his enemies. They intrigued, negotiated, deliberated; pushed forward this man or that; discovered principles, conceived misgivings, procrastinated, and angled for Condé's support; and in all this Rucellai played his part—Rucellai, who hated and feared Richelieu above all men, and to whom the queen must have seemed an ingrate.

In the meantime Bentigovlio was recalled. The Pope had personally recommended Richelieu to the new nuncio; nevertheless, he was little inclined to intercede for him. "He is in a position to tyrannize over all of us," he said. The unending delay made Richelieu ill. His severe headaches returned. But the king himself, urged indeed and persuaded by his mother, now demanded the cardinalate for Richelieu. The ministers were prepared to agree; they required only that he should go to Rome and become a cardinal of the Curia. It was the last thing he thought of doing. He was not thinking of the dignity; for him the red hat meant only a step to political power in his own country. Even afterwards he never made the prescribed journey *ad limina Apostolorum*.

The Government was still confronted by the same problem: to turn against the Habsburgs, whose power was enormously increased, or to continue the civil war as the Catholic party desired. Condé, whatever his reasons, had become a fanatical enemy of the Huguenots, and the war against the Huguenots was continued. But in Rohan the Protestants had a tried and experienced leader. Also the siege of Montpellier, which was now undertaken, made no progress. On the other hand, the great nobles of the party were ready to submit, and old Lesdiguières, who in July had become a Catholic, and in return was appointed Constable, negotiated a peace. In his chagrin Condé left the army and made a pilgrimage to Loretto. The queen, who had again left the Court, now returned thither. The ministers had to give way, and greatly against their will they were now compelled seriously to demand the cardinalate for Richelieu. In Rome they were tired of this everlasting shilly-shallying. The king himself urged the appointment, and on the 25th of September, 1622, Richelieu was at last created cardinal. He is said to have jumped for joy when he received the news. The first great aim of his passionate ambition was fulfilled. From all sides came congratulations: from the Pope, the king, the ministers. He hastened to the Court, in order to return thanks. In Lyons, in the archiepiscopal chapel, the king set the biretta on his head; but Richelieu turned to Marie de' Medici, laid the biretta at her feet, and said: "This purple, which I owe to Your Majesty's benevolence, shall always remind me of my solemn vow to shed my blood in your service." In the evening the new Cardinal gave a dinner to the queen, the princes, and the nobles of the Court.

The events of the next few weeks are not wholly clear. They were of such a nature that the most important transactions were effected by secret conferences and intrigues behind locked doors; it is obvious that such proceedings must often escape cognizance, and at best the reports of them are incomplete and contradictory. What influence was brought to bear on the king we do not know. Many events co-operated. The external situation, which had been neglected, was becoming more and more unfavourable to France. Bavaria was demanding the territory and the electoral dignity of the dispossessed Elector Palatine; whereby a strong Catholic power, which was not that of the Habsburgs, would have pushed its way between the Spanish possessions. In this way England, who was demanding the restoration of the Elector, and Spain were being brought together. The Prince of Wales, accompanied by the Duke of Buckingham, passed through France unrecognized, in order to sue for the hand of a Spanish princess; which in those days of family and cabinet government was an event of far-reaching significance. Naturally, as the Elector was the son-in-law of the English king, a vigorous intercession was made in his favour. Spain had no intention of fulfilling the Treaty of Madrid and of demolishing the forts which controlled the Valtellina; the Grisons were weary of the matter and willing to surrender the passes; and the Archduke Leopold had forced on Switzerland the Treaty of Lindau, by which Chur and Mayenfeld were to receive Austrian garrisons. The encircling of France appeared complete, for the Habsburgs, who five years earlier—in Austria at least—had seemed to be ruined, were now once more at the summit of power.

Schomberg, who had been appointed intendant of finances, was in favour of armed intervention on the part of France, but the ministers were far too timid for such a step. It was agreed to hand over the Valtellina provisionally to the Pope. Schomberg was forced to resign.

Since Luynes' death the young king had so strictly reserved all decisions for himself that the ministers, who by nature were merely over-cautious officials, dared hardly to venture anything, but went to the king at all hours of the day, with every question that came before them, until the young man (he was now two-and-twenty), being thus continually pestered, grew weary of them, fled from them, and went a-hunting, and for more than a year troubled his head about nothing. Now they did whatever they chose. Suddenly the king took charge again, and whoever seemed to dispute his authority was dismissed—a situation which individual ministers exploited to the full against their colleagues.

The Marquis de La Vieuville, who was appointed in Schomberg's place, hustled the old Sillery and his son out of the ministry: their policies were a failure, they had no longer any hold on the Court, and their avarice was altogether too extreme and too successful.

They were dismissed early in February 1624, and for six weeks Vieuville was practically Prime Minister. He attempted to initiate important policies, but he peculated, like his predecessors; he was connected by marriage with unsavoury financiers, and intellectually he was not competent to carry out his own plans; his speech and his dealings were incautious and impetuous, and characterized by a self-confidence which was wholly unjustified, and that arrogant and slightly brutal tone which ambitious men who overrate their own importance are fond of adopting. Beside him, behind him, stood the menacing, imperturbable, and irremovable figure of the slender, elegant priest, compared with whom he was only an empty and vacillating figure-head; whose ideas and opinions, advanced by the queen, were only too striking and too pertinent, and whose influence was increasing from day to day. Since the queen-mother was inexorable in demanding his admission to the privy council, La Vieuville himself at last proposed his inclusion, but in a quality which would leave him without influence on the council's policy; as though such a thing had been possible with a personality so irresistible. The king himself, who under influence of his youthful impressions had so long struggled against him, regarding him as treacherous, dangerous, and domineering, now desired his presence. It is possible that Père Joseph, who had repeatedly spoken of Richelieu, had accustomed the king to the idea of his appointment. Richelieu, however, begged to be excused, on the grounds of his uncertain health, which forced him to live a carefully regulated life; he could not stand for long, could not endure a crowd, and if burdened with other business would not be able to fulfil his obligations as a courtier. When an understanding was arrived at on these points he begged the king, in an earnest and significant letter, that he would support him in this position, which he had not desired, and which he accepted only out of obedience, whatever others might advance against him.

So he became minister, but in a certain sense outside the cabinet. He was taken into the confidence of the council, and his wise opinion was asked, only in so far as La Vieuville approved, for the latter still reserved the power of decision for himself.

In Madrid an attempt had been made to convert the Prince of Wales; the Spaniards demanded the restoration of the Catholic religion in England, and the marriage fell through. The prince now became a suitor for the hand of the Princess Henriette Marie, of France, the sister of Louis XIII. Richelieu demanded only certain alleviations of the position of the English Catholics. This was a ticklish and difficult affair, in which both the Pope and the two parties in France were interested. It was not long before a difference of opinion occurred between Vieuville and Richelieu, in this and in other matters of foreign policy. It is clear that Richelieu could not endure a bungler as his superior where he felt himself to be a master. As in his conflict with Luynes, he set those dangerous writers to work whose ephemeral pamphlets and broadsheets were not without influence at the Court and throughout the country. La Vieuville committed blunder after blunder, and made things easy for him. Richelieu declared that he had warned him, and made excuses for him to the king, but at last it was no longer possible to do so. Doubtless the king was already under the spell which the Cardinal's speeches, which were marked by the profoundest respect, and a ruthless and compelling logic, were weaving about him like a ductile but impenetrable web.

On the 12th of August, 1624, three months after Richelieu's appointment to the council, La Vieuville was dismissed, and since his violence and indiscretion made him formidable, he was imprisoned in the castle of Amboise. On the 13th of August Richelieu was invested with the position, though not as yet with the title, of first minister. He proposed Bochart de Champigny and Marillac as reliable and upright men for the finances, and Schomberg was recalled.

As though in token that a new age was commencing, three men, who in the preceding period had played a leading part, had lately died: the old president, Jeannin, who had for so long been the trusted adviser of Henri IV; the able, valiant, and moderate leader of the Huguenots, Duplessis-Mornay, and the crafty Bouillon, adviser to the Courts of Europe, who, forging and elaborating and obliterating his plans, had played his part in all the political developments of the time.

CHAPTER VII

RICHELIEU'S WORK

From now onwards to his death—for eighteen years—Richelieu remained minister. His work during these eighteen years was decisive for the fate of France and of Europe as that of no other man had been. Those who succeeded him, who completed his work, and from whom the rest of Europe, dazzled by its brilliance, took it over—Mazarin and Louis XIV—were followers in his footsteps.

Not that he had announced a new doctrine or new principles. In the confused relations of the period, as they had developed in the course of the centuries, in the conflict of the forces and classes that were struggling for power, all sorts of opinions were present as latent possibilities. The tendency to absolute sovereignty, the faith in it, the theory of it, were all in existence, particularly in France; and there were also forces, a faith, and a theory which opposed themselves to absolutism. At the cross-roads of these tendencies and opinions Richelieu interposed, and set the course for Europe. He did this in the simple but overpowering desire to translate into fact the knowledge which was his of the actualities of the situation, of the interaction of forces in Europe, and the possibility of diverting them in favour of France. To this end he was obliged to concentrate all the available energies of the nation, and to convert them into a serviceable instrument of his knowledge and his will. And he could enforce his will only as the servant and minister of the king, whose absolute power was at his disposal. Therefore the authority of the king must be as great and complete as possible. For him, therefore, absolutism did not present itself as a theory, but as the natural corollary of his goal, because it was necessary as the means of attaining that goal. Less in theory than in his actual operations, he was moving against the currents of the age, damming them back and diverting them; for the intellectual and political tendencies of the time were making not for absolutism, but for the extension of the incomplete State constitution of the Middle Ages; and with the rise of the bourgeoisie they turned in the direction of democratic constitutionalism, a development which, by reason of the peculiar conditions existing in France, and the interposition of Richelieu, and the impression which his completed work—the monarchy of Louis XIV—made on the Courts of Europe, was checked, subdued, and repressed for two hundred years. In the department of foreign policy he established that hegemony of France in Europe which was likewise to endure for two centuries.

Precisely because his absolutism proceeded from his will rather than from his intellect, because, having to fight from the very beginning, and having taken the helm in circumstances of the greatest urgency, he had never had time to formulate his autocratic propensities in a considered system, he permitted the numerous fragmentary constitutional elements in France to survive. These were so firmly rooted in the past, and in the conceptions of the people, and so bound up with the interests of large and powerful classes, that if he had attempted to abolish them he would only have added enormous difficulties and dangers to those which he already had to face. He contented himself with respecting them as little as possible and preventing their further development. Opposition, wherever it showed itself, he suppressed by force.

A man who is superior to others and knows it, and who is by nature energetic and authoritative, will always incline to autocracy. Such a man should be matched against an exceptional political tradition, and a belief in the justification and authenticity of constitutional institutions, such as is possible only in countries possessing this tradition, and a perfect familiarity with the psychological means by which he can, nevertheless, make his superiority felt, in order to compel the constitution to accommodate itself with docility.

In the France of Richelieu these conditions did not exist, and his character and abilities being what they were, the last thing he would desire would be to seek to create them. It was said in praise of Gustavus Adolphus of Sweden that he had "in a peculiar fashion united and combined two different and indeed almost antithetical things, namely, the liberty of the subject and the greatest possible authority of the sovereign." Richelieu had no thought of attempting any such thing. He served the State, the interests of France. The *raison d'État*—that is, his view of what was desirable for the State—was the deciding factor. What hampered him he sought, if it did not amend itself, to abolish by gentle means or otherwise; most frequently, yielding to his masterful temper, by peremptory and violent means. He could endure and would tolerate no criticism, for that was already a hindrance. "It is desirable," he wrote on the 28th of June, 1626, to the Chevalier du Guet (the "Knight of the Watch"—the old title of the chief of the Paris police), " that everyone should concern himself with his own affairs; and the people who know how to use the pen and write books would be doing the king a great service, and would greatly oblige those who are about him, if they would refrain from speaking either well or ill of their doings, for their praise is often as damaging as their invective. I have begged all those persons of whom I knew that they intended to write in favour of the Government to abstain from so doing." The scorn in the words is evident. But he was not bound by this absolutist view, and throughout his life he made use of the Press, of whose power he was well aware, to influence public opinion; only, the Press must remain an obedient tool of the Government.

It was his opinion that the king was bound to listen to counsel, but this principle is in force even in an Oriental Sultanate. He thought it improper that an individual favourite should possess the ear of the king, so long as Luynes was that favourite. In France it was a time-honoured principle that "the king and his council" governed the country. Richelieu partly transformed the various councils, the number of whose members was restricted, and they nervously endeavoured to give the advice which he wished to hear; and anyone who did not do so, or gave unsuitable advice, was prejudicing his own interests.

The Parlements continued to exist, but if they meddled in politics, or criticized the policy of the ministers, or refused to register decrees, he saw to it that they were informed by the king that such conduct would not be tolerated. At the close of his life, in his *Political Testament*, he spoke in very severe terms of the power of this hereditary class of officials, who were, as a matter of fact, too selfish to represent the people and too weak to offer any real resistance, yet strong enough to be inconvenient and disturbing. However, he obstructed them even in their most useful function, and that which they fulfilled for the most part honourably—that of administering justice. "In the opinion of all the doctors," we read in an early portion of his so-called *Mémoires*, "the kings never grant a privilege against themselves, so that no privilege can deprive the kings of complete freedom to make use of their authority to punish the guilty." It was thus that he justified arbitrary interference in matters of jurisdiction. Such expressions, which may certainly be traced back to his own utterances, and out of which one might construct a theory of absolutism, are of frequent occurrence in his letters as in the *Mémoires*. In one of the last and most important edicts registered on the 21st of February, 1641, in a *lit de justice*, we find this principle expressed: "Just as the absolute authority of the monarch raises the States to the summit of fame, even so in a short space of time we behold them fall if this authority is weakened." The States-General were not again convoked under Richelieu. The Notables were assembled once, shortly after he entered upon office; they were at once given to understand that their assembly must be of brief duration, and in a draft of Richelieu's of the order of the day there is mention of "the only too frequent instances of disobedience in this country." Since his will and his whole personality were autocratic, his views found expression not only in his actions, but quite as frequently in his words as well.

His views of life, as well as his procedure, were from the very first inherent in the nature of the man, and in the situation by which he was confronted it was inevitable that his strategy should develop along this line.

He came into power in August 1624. In the fourteen years since the death of Henri IV everything had become thoroughly confused. Internally, France had become disorganized; the great nobles had again recovered their ominous power in the State; in the south the semi-republican organization of the Huguenots, dangerously defiant and fanatical, had become "a State within the State"; and, what with a common faith and ancient memories, it had repeatedly given signs of a reviving inclination towards England, under whose rule the south had lived for centuries. In matters of foreign policy the house of Habsburg was once more all-powerful. Spain had world-power and sea-power, and, like England in the nineteenth century, the Spanish Government grasped at the symbol of this dominion: she demanded that the Pope should confer on the King of Spain the title of "Emperor of India." The Pope saw himself in danger of becoming "a domestic chaplain of the Habsburgs."

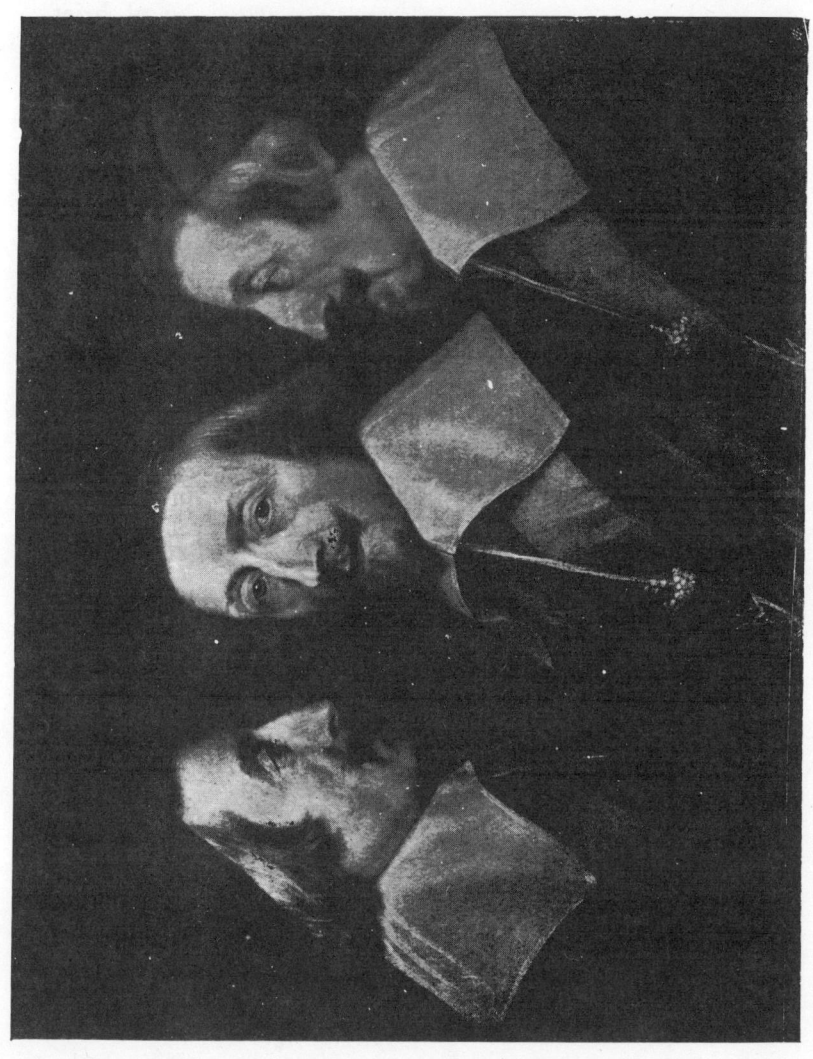

THREE HEADS OF RICHELIEU
(Philippe de Champaigne. *British Museum*)

The Swiss passes which France had so long controlled were in Spanish and Austrian hands; by the Treaty of Prague (March 30, 1613) the Archduke Ferdinand had promised to cede Alsace to the Spaniards, in return for their support in the election to the Imperial throne. The encirclement of France was rapidly nearing completing. All this was seen and recognized by Richelieu; all this he had doubtless expounded to the king with his compelling yet insinuating logic.

Shortly before his death, in the introduction to his *Political Testament*, he wrote: "I promised Your Majesty to apply all my faculties and all the authority which you would vouchsafe to confer on me to destroying the Huguenot party, humbling the power of the great, recalling all your subjects to their duty, and exalting Your Majesty's name among the foreign nations to that height which is its due." He must at least have actually said something of the sort.

When he came into power he was scarcely known in France; his brief ministry in the time of the Maréchal d'Ancre had not created any great sensation, and after the lapse of seven years was hardly remembered by the multitude. His situation was one which occurs in the lives of most great men, though its duration varies; he was known and appreciated by a small circle, but as good as unknown to the bulk of the people. Now he stands forth almost alone in his lonely grandeur; then he was one among twenty million Frenchmen, one man at a turbulent and unsettled Court, and no one had less faith than the Court in the permanence of his government. He had come into power through the influence of the queen-mother; he was accounted "her creature"; he called himself so; he had come forward as the hope of the Spanish and Catholic party, because he was an ecclesiastic and a good Catholic, and the queen belonged to this party, and because his appointment had been amiably received in Rome; but even the other party, the party of the "good Frenchmen," had hopes of him, because their spokesmen believed that they understood him and his opinions.

He was surrendered by a throng of men of all qualities, outwardly polite and submissive; the princes and great nobles, every one of whom felt himself to be infinitely his superior; Monsieur, the brother of the king; Condé (but he at first was still absent from the Court), and the Comte de Soissons—all of them ambitious, and in the hands of even more ambitious advisers; from the haughty magnates like Épernon, Guise, and Montmorency, down to the petty nobles and the Abbés, a mob of active, wide-awake, covetous, and malevolent persons, greedy for power, place, and influence, each of them convinced that he was qualified for every office, and to form a judgment upon every matter; most of them old in intrigue and conspiracy; the stiff-necked but no less ambitious and cultivated jurists of the Parlements and law-courts, who felt themselves to be qualified *ex officio* for the task of administration; and the foreign envoys, who kept a watch on the doings of the new minister, and reckoned up their ability to influence him. And the ladies of the Court; the queen-mother, and the young queen, neglected by her listless husband, but surrounded by influential old ladies, and old ladies who claimed to be influential, and by young and beautiful women, and the men whom they twisted round their fingers; all of whom discussed, every evening, the man who now held the reins; praising or disapproving, accordingly as every move he made did or did not further their own petty personal schemes.

And hitherto the young minister—he had not yet completed his thirty-ninth year—the young Cardinal with the long, sickly face, the thin lips, and the small, pointed beard, encountered everyone with equal, smiling courtesy, obsequious, for all the distinction of his bearing, with the fawning amiability of a great supple cat, whose dangerous character is not yet realized by his victims. As yet men did not fear him; as yet the most important factor of power, the conviction that he was powerful, the fear and the faith that paralyse, had not been evoked in the minds of those who surrounded him. As yet he was a minister, as others had been before him. But he knew that he was surrounded by masks which hid the faces of enemies; that almost all men, from the very first, were anticipating his imminent downfall. And a man who went his own way as consciously and inexorably as did Richelieu could not please even his few friends.

There was one man who could hold out against him, whom he absolutely must have on his side—the king. He had learned this from his first downfall. From the day of his appointment as minister Richelieu was the king's man, and no longer Marie de' Medici's as hitherto. But this the queen did not realize.

RICHELIEU

In the French archives is a document in the hand of Richelieu's private secretary, Le Masle, and supplemented in many places by his secretary, Charpentier, and by himself. It was written in the first or second week of January 1629, and contains a character-sketch of Louis XIII. Richelieu was accustomed to keep a written account of the political situation, his plans, and the general outlook, in which he weighed facts and possibilities and the consequences of every possible step, and such documentary expositions served as a preparation for his proposals to the king and for any important transactions. In this document we read: "The king is kindly, virtuous, silent, and loves glory, but one may truly say that he is often too impetuous; he is also suspicious, jealous, and prone to passing excitement; he concerns himself too much with trivialities, and is at times ill-tempered. . . .", and all these qualities, with their consequences, are thoroughly discussed. The astonishing thing is that the Cardinal told the king all that was thus written down, and not when he was alone with him, but in the presence of his mother and his confessor, Père Suffren. He concluded by saying that for all these reasons he feared that he would be unable to retain the king's favour; and on this account, and because of his bad health, he begged the king to give him leave to resign, which was refused. Now, for the first time since his first extraordinary success—the conquest of La Rochelle—he seems to have ventured to play for the highest stake. The king listened to him with great patience and promised to take all his lessons to heart.

Louis XIII is a tragic figure: a man of peculiar character, somehow undeveloped, or developed awry. He was simple and by no means exigent, although thoroughly kingly in his bearing, and very conscious of his dignity and power; yet he was by nature shy, easily influenced, and unable to oppose those who had once obtained influence over him. He was by no means intellectual; his sympathies were narrow; he had little learning, and was not fond of learning; yet he was not without a certain natural intelligence and power of judgment. He read practically nothing; he had all sorts of odd talents for all sorts of manual work, for cooking, gardening, and mason's work; he knew how to handle almost any kind of tool; he could forge and weld and make castings; he drew and painted; he could play almost any instrument; he was a composer, and had always chamber-music at his call. He was an excellent rider and a good shot; no commander, but a fine soldier, with a thorough knowledge and understanding of all things military; he could be affectionate, kindly, and grateful; in the depths of his heart he really was so; he was just in intention and by nature, but was hard and pitiless when his authority was impugned, and in cases of disloyalty. His sisters, particularly the lovely Elizabeth, known in the family circle as Mignonette, who did not feel at her ease in the stiff Spanish Court, and longed to return to the cheerful freedom of France, loved him dearly. To his governess, Madame de Monglat, whom he and his sisters always addressed by the old childish nickname of "Mamanga," he continued to write affectionate and grateful letters. But early disappointments had embittered his affectionate and childlike nature; they, too, were responsible for his impediment of speech, and an internal complaint which early made its appearance. He seemed incapable of sensuous pleasure, and he grew up into a sad and melancholy man. The painful events which had occurred in his own family; the timid reserve which made it impossible for him to express and unburden himself, so that he shut up his anger and bitterness within himself, and suffered from them for years; and, added to this, his consciousness of the superiority of the great and powerful man whom he had to keep beside him and tolerate—all this may have contributed to his melancholy. Secretly conscious, perhaps, that he was overburdened by his task, and feeling that nothing could ever be as he wished, that he could never in anything have his own way, he became increasingly morose and peculiar as the years went by. What Richelieu meant and was accomplishing for him and for France he knew well enough; and it was characteristic of him that he held fast to anyone to whom he had at one time clung, and even though something within him rebelled against the man, or though he was weary of him, he could not bring himself to get rid of him. Only when another succeeded in obtaining the mastery over his mind and wrenching him away did he throw over his favourites; then he did so quickly enough. This Richelieu knew, and he was able to protect both the king and himself. He remained always near the king, however it might fatigue him and waste his time; he was loth to leave him, and when reasons of State or some caprice of the king's made separation inevitable, he saw to it that intelligent and reliable men, who were entirely devoted to him, should remain with the king; and these men had to send him daily reports of the king's every thought and emotion, of every peevish remark; and day by day they received their instructions as to what they were to say to the king. Since Richelieu himself was too great and superior a man to be a favourite in the sense of becoming the king's daily companion, and was, moreover, too overburdened with work, there were always ladies and gentlemen who kept him company, and gained peculiar favour by taking part in his modest and often curious amusements, such as sketching, music, shoemaking, preserving fruits, or imitating the faces of the dying—for that was one of the strange entertainments in which he and his courtiers indulged in later years—and, above all, hunting, in which the invalidish minister was never able to join him. These courtiers in particular the Cardinal had kept under observation; and they had to be completely subservient to him, or they were inexorably removed from the king's vicinity, if need be by the most insidious and deliberate intrigues. Amidst the vast and wearing anxieties of an intricate policy, the most difficult business of the cabinet, and great military enterprises, he was compelled incessantly to safeguard his only point of support; to take thought of such matters, and never for a moment to lose sight of the feeble, irresolute, and unreliable source of his authority. He sought to circumscribe him entirely, and although in those days, at a great and critical moment, he had permitted himself to censure the king, at other times he did not fail to pay him the utmost homage, to flatter him to the top of his bent. "The king is the ablest member of his council," he constantly repeated; and especially in the beginning he contrived so to frame his proposals that the king, though compelled to arrive at Richelieu's conclusions, believed that he had deduced them for himself. In public, and in the sessions of the Parlement, he lauded the king for being the very last thing he was or could be, "the real leader of his government," under whose rule miracles were performed. But when these wonderful things were accomplished he never failed to point to his own services and their successful issue, and to ensure that others alluded to them. Here was a task for his friends and helpers, and they were well aware that they must perform it. The enduring and ever-recurring motive by which he could produce the strongest impression on the king, and win him to his purposes, was the thought that he, Louis XIII, was "a great king," and must behave as such, and that he, Richelieu, was by his services procuring him the rank of a great monarch. But for all his ease he could never feel quite secure. Despite his successes, despite the king's conviction of his ability, despite a personal subjection which went so far that the king's words, and his marginal comments on the documents laid before him, were merely the obedient echo of the voice of his powerful minister; there were many occasions on which Louis became restive, and at times he was filled with a burning hatred of the man of whose superiority he was only too conscious. So, to the end of the minister's life, there existed a deep-rooted yet suspicious and insecure

LOUIS XIII
(Philippe de Champaigne. *Louvre, Paris*)

RICHELIEU'S WORK

friendship between the two men, and on this friendship Richelieu's power was based.

He must, above all things, have feared that if the king were to die—and he was never well, and often seriously ill—he, too, would be lost. His intense and strenuous activity was dependent on the life and humour of a weakly and capricious master; it hung by a thread which threatened every day to break. Richelieu began to provide for a certain personal wealth and power. As a poor nobleman and cleric he had felt his poverty severely. Since his position now offered him possibilities of providing for himself he profited by them. He received rich benefices from the king, who in general was niggardly and by no means fond of giving, as rewards for his services. He did not snatch at wealth, as Concini did before him and Mazarin after; he had a regard for appearances; and when the king wished to confer on him the feudal fiefs of the Grand Prior of Vendôme, who, on Richelieu's advice, had been arrested and had died in prison, he declined them. But he began with an income of 25,000 livres and landed property of about the same value, and when he had been ten years a minister this income had risen to 500,000 livres, and later still it had increased even more enormously.

As his power increased he filled as many posts as possible with persons who were subservient to him, and whenever he could do so he prevented the advancement of such as were not useful to him personally. When he was obliged to appoint princes of the Royal house or great nobles as governors and army leaders, they were surrounded and watched by his familiars.

He drew up lists of the men who seemed to him trustworthy, or whom he could not pass over. Such a list, containing about two hundred names, arranged according to their provinces and their callings, is still extant. Those whom he knew to be wholly devoted to him he promoted, for he was grateful to loyalty, and looked for it. M. de St. Georges, as captain of Concini's guards, was the only man who had offered any resistance when his master was murdered; Richelieu, mindful of his behaviour, gave him the same post in his own service, for the menacing hatred aroused by his ruthless procedure soon forced him to maintain a bodyguard of his own.

He employed in the first place the old friends and adherents of his family from Poitou; and then the Bouthilliers, Claude and his son Léon, whom he made Comte de Chavigny, and for whom he had a special affection. His letters to Chavigny, which touch upon the most important and delicate State secrets, and contain confidential instructions for the management and observation of the king, are written in the more cheerful tone for which, in addressing the very few in whom he had perfect confidence, he abandoned his logical austerity and matter-of-fact frigidity. Richelieu's attempts to be jocular were heavy and unpleasing, as is often the case with excessively austere people. But in his letters to Chavigny, whom he used to call "Monsieur Junior," we find a freer and more amiable tone. For that matter it was rumoured at Court, and the gossips of Paris agreed, that Chavigny was his natural son. This was doubtless a calumny; the relevant dates show the relationship to be quite improbable. The Bouthilliers were old and trusted friends, and both father and son became secretaries of State and Richelieu's most intimate agents in the task of government. Another such agent was the zealous and impetuous Père Joseph, who meddled with everything and thrust himself forward everywhere, and was derided by many for his gloomy pathos. Richelieu held him in check, yet greatly valued him; he became that "Grey Eminence" whom the minister called his Ezekiel, or, jestingly, the *Tenebroso Cavernoso*, who was frequently employed as envoy, and in 1634 was also appointed minister. A host of officers and officials, men of the first families of France, and others of the humblest origin, with Germans, Scotsmen, and Italians, were more or less in Richelieu's service. Monks came and went incessantly—they were his spies. The Church, the army, the administration, and society were more and more penetrated by his creatures. Those who did not support him out of admiration and inclination, or shrewdness, or fear, he attempted to buy. This inexorable schemer made use of all and every means: his will, and only his will, must be accomplished in France; and to those who were not amenable, who rebelliously sought to go their own way, or even went over to his enemies, he showed no mercy. Many did so for one reason or another; because their opinions were not his, or for party reasons; hoping to reap an apparent profit, or seduced by promises, or by women; they helped his enemies and opposed his schemes—and fell, suddenly and dreadfully, when they least expected it.

As a matter of course he benefited and promoted

his relatives; the Richelieu family became one of the greatest in France. The men became cardinals, dukes, admirals, marshals; the women were married into the greatest families.

All that he was planning and building up needed time for its realization. In the beginning he had nothing but the uncertain confidence of the king and the faith of a few lesser men to set against the envy, aversion, and distrust or disdain of the majority; nothing, save his own extraordinary assurance, his unconquerable will.

So he began the campaign against the Royal family, the nobles, the parties, the bourgeoisie, and the whole of hostile Europe.

CHAPTER VIII

THE FIRST BATTLES WITH THE COURT

As a result of the timid and incapable policy of Richelieu's predecessors, France had completely lost the respect of Europe. "Is there a king in France?" asked the Elector Johann Georg of Saxony of the French envoy, M. de Marescot; and when the latter retorted: "A great and powerful king!" the Elector replied: "That is curious! Could there really have been a powerful king of France, and we for four years never to have noticed it?"

The Spaniards had no intention of renouncing the Valtellina passes; so long as the Pope kept them garrisoned they were open to them in case of need, and the Pope would not restore the Catholic valley to the Protestant Grisons. Richelieu commenced his negotiations, and, as nothing came of them, he sent some French troops across the Alps in the depth of winter, under the command of the Marquis de Cœuvres, afterwards the Maréchal d'Estrées, to the aid of the Grisons. This assistance of an allied power was not reckoned an act of war by the current law of nations. Cœuvres took the forts and drove the Papal troops out of the valley, although in other respects he treated them with courtesty and consideration. In order to keep the Spaniards busy on the western frontier of the duchy the Duke of Savoy attacked Genoa, supported, as the ally of France, by Lesdiguières; and since a Spanish army under Spinola had undertaken the resubjection of the Netherlands, Richelieu supported the latter and Count Mansfield with money. At the same time he opened negotiations with Denmark, and the Princess Henriette Marie was betrothed to the Prince of Wales; which seemed to be the most important step of all.

This was a Protestant policy, and the Catholics at once became uneasy. Thereupon—at the most unfortunate time for themselves—the Huguenots in France revolted. Soubise, the Hotspur of the pary , occupied the Île de Ré and captured some ships; the Duc de Rohan called upon his co-religionists to rise. In the greatest indignation over the interference with his policy Richelieu described the two brothers as "The Antichrist"; once more they proved to him that "so long as the Huguenots had power in France the king could never be master in his country, nor could anything glorious be undertaken abroad." His plans matured, and he perceived his task more clearly than ever. This was the time when religion was beginning to lose its power as the strongest of all political motives, and the national interests were beginning to be paramount. But as yet these motive forces were entangled. France had no navy, and while England and Holland lent the king ships to use against the sea-going French Protestants, there was no relying on their Protestant captains and crews. Nevertheless, the Duc de Montmorency, the French admiral, was victorious over Soubise, though he had but very few ships of his own; but, thanks to his brilliance and his lovable character, he was able to carry the Dutch with him, while others

THE FIRST BATTLES WITH THE COURT

he compelled by threats. The result was a mutiny in Amsterdam, and the Dutch auxiliary fleet was recalled. Meanwhile Cardinal Barberini had come to Paris as Papal legate, in order to negotiate peace in Italy. At the same time the Duke of Buckingham, the favourite and minister of Charles I, had come from England to escort the French princess to London. He was anxious to conclude an alliance with France, in order to wage a common war against Spain and to reinstate the Elector Palatine, who was the king of England's son-in-law. The presence of the legate made the Huguenots fear that peace might be concluded with Spain, when the Government would be able to proceed against them with all its forces. The Spanish Government feared that the presence of Buckingham portended a peace with the Huguenots and an alliance between France and England, which would enable France to intervene with redoubled energy in Italy and the Netherlands. Richelieu, with amazing dexterity, succeeded in profiting by the reciprocal fears of both opponents, and concluding a not unfavourable peace with both. It was his ingenious method to derive an advantage from a twofold necessity and danger, by exploiting the one against the other. The situation of France was improved; the passes, when the treaty was carried out, would again be in French hands, and the Powers were beginning to feel the hand of a supreme statesman.

These great European events had loomed up against a petty background; from a web of personal intrigues, which were continued as before, the threads ran into the region of politics. No one at Court could as yet surmise what the new minister meant to them and to France; Marie de' Medici and her adherents had already more than once become powerful in her son's Court, and had again been supplanted. The Royal family, with the exception of the queen-mother, consisted almost entirely of inexperienced young people; and while at the Court of the old, domineering, embittered Marie de' Medici there was no talk of anything but religion and politics, the Court of the "little queen" Anne was full of jesting and chattering voices; but even the young women meddled in politics. The most childlike unsuspicion confronted the ingenious will which was on the eve of creating a new France.

Louis XIII had been married as a child. He was a dark-skinned, pretty, slender boy. He was not strongly sensual, and women had not much attraction for him; he had passionate friendships with men. Moreover, his extraordinary bashfulness held him back, and for a long while his early marriage was not consummated. The European Courts became aware of the fact. There was a considerable exchange of dispatches on the subject between the Court at Madrid and the Spanish envoy in Paris and the French Cabinet; there were long discussions between the queen's confessor and the Papal nuncio. Remarkable things happened, and the foreign envoys wrote curious reports for their Governments. When Louis' half-sister, Mlle. de Vendôme, married the Duc d'Elbœuf, she showed the king, who had never ventured into his wife's bed, "how nuptials were celebrated." Only then did the young king summon up his courage; the marriage

ANNE OF AUSTRIA
(Rubens. *Prado, Madrid*)

THE FIRST BATTLES WITH THE COURT

was consummated; a brief time of happiness followed, and the queen had hope of issue. Apart from one or two more elderly ladies of honour she was surrounded by young and high-spirited women. A woman who had some influence with the queen was the gifted, ambitious, and conscienceless Princess de Conti, then about forty years of age, referred to in the cipher-letters exchanged by Richelieu and the king as "la peché"; another, who had even more, was the handsome, foolish, seductive widow of the Connétable de Luynes, Marie de Rohan. Always thirsting for fresh sensations, she brought disaster and disorder wherever she went; herself precociously corrupted, she gave the queen indecent books to read. The handsome grand master of the horse, the Duc de Bellegarde, and the brilliant young Montmorency, paid harmless court to the "little queen." Wild and frolicsome, the young women romped about the halls of the Louvre. One evening the queen fell down, injured herself, and had a miscarriage. Greatly angered, the king ordered the immediate removal of these thoughtless ladies, and of the Duchesse de Luynes. The young queen wrote an offended reply and refused to obey. The king insisted upon having his way. Thus began an estrangement between the husband and the wife, both of whom were sensitive and resentful. Mme. de Luynes had no desire to live in banishment and disgrace, and required the Duc de Chevreuse, a prince of the house of Lorraine, who had long been her lover, to marry her. He was very greatly her senior, and could not withstand her. With his help, and that of Bassompierre, who succeeded in winning the king over, she returned to the Court and the queen. In October 1613 Louis, who once more noted her influence with displeasure, in order to get rid of her, abolished for good and all the office which she then filled of grand mistress of the queen's household. The queen wept, but he remained inexorable. His attitude towards his wife became cold and imperious, while hers towards him was haughty and inimical. Since Marie de' Medici had returned to the Court there were disputes between her and the young queen over the matter of precedence, and encroachments on one another's privileges, and incessant quarrels, which were often so violent that the king had to compose them. All this increased the estrangement of husband and wife, and, in spite of all he could do, the king had not succeeded in actually removing Mme. de Chevreuse. The two women, who had formed the closest intimacy, were united against him.

Meanwhile the question of the English betrothal had begun to occupy the Court and the two Governments; the Duc de Chevreuse in particular had exerted himself to bring it about, and when the Prince of Wales, having through the death of his father become king as Charles I, was detained in England, Chevreuse was given the honourable task of marrying the Princess Henriette Marie as his proxy. Now festivity followed festivity; the two ambassadors, the Earls of Holland and Carlisle, who were to conduct the princess to England, went in and out of the palace of the Duc de Chevreuse in the Rue Saint-Thomas-du-Louvre; the handsome, affected Lord Holland was before long the lover of the duchess, and he and

THE FIRST BATTLES WITH THE COURT

Chevreuse conceived the idea, which to them seemed the acme of stagecraft, of bringing about a love affair between the Duke of Buckingham and Queen Anne, whose marriage was once more joyless, their object being to draw still tighter the political bonds uniting the two countries. Buckingham had accordingly appeared on the scene under the pretext of making the final arrangements. Richelieu had not wished him to come, for he thought the man vain and impolitic, but as he could not prevent him from coming he profited by his advent to accomplish a piece of brilliant political double-dealing.

But the duke, immoderately flattered by the thought of conquering a queen, fell seriously in love with Anne; he made a most splendid appearance, enchanting all the women, and the long conversations in which the queen and he became absorbed produced a great impression. Meanwhile the new Queen of England had to start upon her journey; the whole Court escorted her as far as Boulogne, whence a richly decorated ship of State, surrounded by a gaily beflagged fleet, was to carry her to England. As yet Buckingham had accomplished nothing. In the park at Amiens the Duchesse de Chevreuse contrived that he should be left alone with the queen, but he was too impetuous, and the queen called loudly for help. On another occasion he forced his way into her bedroom and threw himself down on her bed; the ladies forced him to leave the room; the queen was silent, but the wooing of the handsome and magnificent nobleman had none the less made a great impression on her. For the French Court the matter had results of the first importance. Louis XIII was secretly informed of all that had happened—some of his informants being spiteful while others sought to excuse the duke—and was furious. Never again, despite all his efforts, did Buckingham receive permission to set foot on the soil of France, and the personal embitterment of the English favourite had serious political consequences.

Since the king had no children, and his feeble health did not promise long life, his seventeen-year-old brother, Gaston, Duc d'Anjou, later Duc d'Orléans, was heir to the throne. While Louis XIII was silent, reserved, and virtuous, Monsieur—for such was Anjou's title—was cheerful, witty, and good-natured though eternally changeable; he had no inward stability, and was cowardly, and precociously dissipated; his nights he spent in drinking, or in visiting houses of ill-fame, which gave rise to serious scandals. The queen-mother loved him better than her eldest son, and could not conceal her preference. Louis XIII was jealous. The younger brother was conscious of his importance as heir to the throne, and the nobles about him, seeking to flatter him, excited his ambition.

Marie de' Medici wanted to marry him to the Princesse de Montpensier, a daughter of the Duchesse de Guise by her first marriage, and the richest heiress of France. She had always desired this match; she loved the princess, who was gracious and lovable, and the reigning line must have heirs; the throne must not pass to the Condés. The house of Condé was, of course, opposed to the marriage, and so was the young

THE FIRST BATTLES WITH THE COURT

Comte de Soissons, who himself wished to make this wealthy match; the queen was by no means anxious to be cast into the shade by a sister-in-law who might become the mother of the future heir to the throne; and even the king had jealous doubts. Richelieu, after protracted consideration and thorough discussion, decided in favour of the betrothal, which was accordingly concluded; perhaps because he thought it desirable, perhaps because, where he himself was in doubt, he did not care to oppose the queen-mother. Meanwhile Mme. de Chevreuse returned from England, whither she and her husband had accompanied Queen Henrietta Maria, and where she scandalized the French ambassador, Comte Tillières, who reported the matter to the Court, by staying in the house of her lover, Lord Holland. She had what she believed to be the best of reasons against this betrothal, and the best idea for the future: Monsieur should remain unmarried, so that when the king died he could marry Anne of Austria, who would then really be queen of France, and would herself be the mother of the heir to the throne. That the Cardinal desired the betrothal seemed to her unimportant; the ladies thought the pretensions of the minister-prelate ridiculous, and did not regard him as dangerous.

Richelieu was sensible of this opposition. In those days he had still to proceed cautiously. It is related that he himself had made love to the queen and sought to win her. This is completely incredible. The rumour may have arisen because he presumably thought it necessary to pay court to the queen, and since he did not do so with the ease of a cavalier, and since his ever-active intellect gave his gallantries a ponderous quality, the women laughed at him. Richelieu was not without traces of foppishness; he liked to play the courtier and the man of letters, and to show himself before the ladies in cavalier dress, just as he liked to appear as a soldier in harness and gauntlets.

He knew that Gaston's plastic temperament was controlled by the confidant of the moment, who at that time was his tutor, the Corsican Colonel d'Ornano. He was promoted to marshal. But the influence of the beautiful Princesse de Condé, with whom the ugly and impetuous old man was in love, and that of the pretty Mme. de Chevreuse was stronger. Instead of persuading the prince to marry, it made him resolve to overthrow Richelieu. The marshal and the two ladies did what all conspirators had done since the death of Henri IV: they proceeded to get into touch with the Prince de Condé, the Comte de Soissons, the two Vendômes, the Duc de Nevers, and the Duc de Longueville, all of whom were ready to co-operate with them. Gaston was to leave Paris and proceed to one of the frontier fortresses; Mme. de Chevreuse negotiated with the Huguenots through her Protestant relative, the Duchesse de Rohan; and alliances were concluded with the Governments of Savoy, Spain, and England. Whether, in the case of successful rebellion and civil war, it was intended to remove not only Richelieu, but the king as well, is uncertain. As always, there were people who tattled or betrayed themselves; Richelieu was well served by his spies and other tools. On the 4th of May, 1626, Ornano

THE FIRST BATTLES WITH THE COURT

was arrested at Fontainebleau, by the captain of the guards, Hallier, who was Vitry's brother, and taken to the fortress of Vincennes. This happened late in the evening; Gaston, who asked leave to speak to the king, was not received. Next morning he met the chancellor d'Aligre, who did not dare to justify the warrant of arrest to the angry prince. Richelieu, to whom he immediately spoke of the matter, coolly accepted all the responsibility. The prince, hurling at him a coarse term of abuse, rushed out of his presence. The chancellor, who had shown himself deficient in energy, was immediately dismissed, and the Seal was entrusted to Michel de Marillac, a confidant of the queen-mother.

Mme. de Chevreuse, who at first was greatly alarmed, had what she considered another of her happy thoughts: the young Marquis de Chalais, of the house of Talleyrand, master of the wardrobe to the king, was in love with her; if nothing else could be done he must murder Richelieu. This extremely handsome but not very intelligent young man took the Commander de Valençay into his confidence: the Commander threatened to tell Richelieu everything, unless Chalais himself would do so. Chalais went to the king. Now Monsieur lost courage and begged that he might be forgiven; Richelieu accepted his submission and dictated the conditions: he drafted a solemn declaration to which the prince must swear at the altar, "before the living image of Him who punishes perjury," to eternal loyalty, and he must report every word which was whispered to him of the conspiracy. Thereupon the king promised him his forgiveness, and Marie de' Medici, weeping, besought her two sons to be united in future. A document was drafted which all three signed. After this extraordinary scene in the Louvre, which, on the king at all events, made a great impression, Richelieu submitted his resignation, which was not accepted. He then betook himself with the king to Brittany, where the two Vendômes were arming. They were summoned to Blois, were there arrested in their beds and conveyed to the fortress of Amboise. The Prince de Condé, with the keen scent of the man who considers his own advantage before anything else on earth, recognized that there was now a man at the head of affairs against whom it was not good to fight: he begged for permission to visit the Cardinal, paid him the most flattering compliments, and declared himself his friend.

The women, however, did not abandon the struggle; Mme. de Chevreuse succeeded in again winning over the unhappy Chalais, and both brought their influence to bear upon Gaston. The prince was to flee to Metz, where the Duc de La Valette was in command. Chalais sent a courier to Metz. He had no idea that Richelieu was having him watched; meanwhile the Court proceeded to Nantes. There Richelieu sent for Chalais, and drove him into a corner; he had intended to escape with the prince on racehorses, but the roads were already guarded, and before the attempt could be made he had been arrested.

On the 2nd of August the king set up a special tribunal of judges, appointed by commission and selected by the Cardinal, who condemned Chalais to

THE DUKE OF BUCKINGHAM
(Rubens. *Pitti, Florence*)

death. Mme. de Chevreuse and seven more nobles were indicted, but nevertheless remained at liberty. Chalais completely lost his nerve, confessed everything, and begged for his life. Monsieur's behaviour was still more pitiful; he betrayed all his friends, agreed to all that was required of him, and was even ready to marry, if offered a sufficiently rich appanage, as to the amount of which there was a great deal of haggling. In vain the queen and Mme. de Chevreuse begged him on their knees not to agree to the marriage; his courage was at an end.

On the 5th of August the parish priest was summoned to the castle, and the betrothal of Mlle. de Montpensier was announced before him and the Cardinal, and on the next day the marriage was hastily celebrated, without festivities, music, or guests, and the Cardinal blessed the married pair.

On the 18th of August, Chalais, the grandson of President Jeannin and the Maréchal de Montluc, was sentenced to death, and on the following day was beheaded in the market-place. In vain his mother pleaded for mercy on her only son. His foolish friends, in the endeavour to save him, had removed the executioner from the city; but this did not delay the inexorable man in the background, who defeated his opponents at every step, and enforced and accomplished his will; the only result was that the execution was unskilfully and horribly performed.

"I have made a necessary journey," stammered the king when, on the 7th of September, he returned to Paris and was greeted by the representatives of the corporation. "It was not very agreeable to me, for I had to act with severity; but there are occasions on which one is forced to do that which one would rather not do."

No proceedings were taken against the heir to the throne, and Mme. de Chevreuse was merely banished from the Court. "One cannot uproot them all," wrote the Cardinal in a memorandum, "for many of them are of such high nobility that one cannot think of punishing them. They continually inflame the relatives of those whom one chastises, and the women will not give over their madness." The insane frivolity of the great nobles of the day is completely exposed by the history of this senseless plot, and the childish struggle of unsuspecting women against the terrible superman. When Mme. de Chevreuse was informed of her banishment she was beside herself to think that anyone should dare to proceed against her on account of such trifles. "The king is an idiot," she blustered, "and allows this buffoon of a Cardinal to give him orders!" But she would show them who she was!

While rage and bewilderment prevailed among the defeated, the conqueror sat ailing in his study, tortured by his eternal headaches and attacks of fever, and oppressed by anxieties on every hand. We can picture him seated with the fateful ciphers of his confidants before him, considering the next step to be taken. *Secretissime* is written on these pages. "It has been learned, by the most secret means, from the mouth of the coupled gods (?), who have opportunity of knowing it, that Chesnelle (Queen Anne) believes that she can marry Hébertin (Monsieur), that she has long hoped . . ." and then follow details of the rôle to be played by "la Chevrette," and of the other persons who were taking part in the affair. These reports were intended for the king.

In his mother's presence Louis reproached his wife with her treachery. She denied everything; by such an exchange, she said, she would gain too little. At the same time she complained bitterly that her friends had been taken from her, and vehemently reproached the queen-mother for persecuting her, with the aid of her creature, the Cardinal, and spoiling her life. But the king did not believe her; he turned away, morosely, and she remained in disgrace.

On the 2nd of September the Maréchal d'Ornano, who was ill when he was arrested, died in prison. At Court and among the populace there was, of course, talk of poison, and there was even more talk of it when the Grand Prior de Vendôme likewise died in prison of a heavy sickness. His brother, the Duc de Vendôme, spent four years in the fortress. Men were beginning to fear the minister.

"If anything were to happen to Calori"—that is, to himself—he remarked at the close of a memorial to the king, "the service would suffer greatly: firstly, because the king would lose a person whom certain persons wish out of the way only because he hinders the wicked schemes of others; secondly, because people would believe that the king is not powerful enough to protect his servants." Thereupon the king granted him a bodyguard of fifty noblemen. In the following year the Prince de Condé visited him at his château of Richelieu. They discussed the past and the future, and once more the prince expressed his admiration of the Cardinal. When the prince had gone the Cardinal recorded the gist of their conversation in high-sounding phrases. At the end of the memorandum is a comment in his own hand: "Condé will play no more foolish tricks."

CHAPTER IX

LA ROCHELLE

EVEN while Richelieu was conducting the intricate peace negotiations with the Huguenots and with Spain, and while he was still threatened by these dangerous happenings at Court, yet other difficulties had arisen. The century-old ecclesiastical and political dispute of the jurists and theologians had again flared up. The Sorbonne and the Paris Parlement had condemned a whole series of publications, and in particular a work by the Jesuit father Santarelli, who had lately been teaching the doctrine that the Pope had the right to dethrone kings and even to condemn them to death. The Parlement and University were defending the "liberties of the Gallican Church," which were, as a matter of fact, limitations of ecclesiastical power. Once again they had come into conflict with the Orders, and above all with the Jesuits, and with the bishops also, over the most hotly contested principles of Gallicanism: that in France the Pope should have no power in temporal matters; that in France his infallibility should not be recognized; and that the king's council was above the Pope. Protests and appeals to the council followed. For Richelieu these were ticklish questions. He was a Cardinal of the Roman Church, and he was a French minister; he was not willing to surrender the king's prerogatives, yet he could not quarrel with the Church and the Catholic party. The nuncio, Monsignore Spada, had already broken off relations with him, and in Rome the feeling towards him was by no means so friendly as it had been. And he was once more in need of the support of Rome; to begin with, in respect of the Valtellina problem. Also he did not want to make enemies of the Jesuits, although he was far from loving them. He attempted, therefore, to stifle the dispute instead of settling it, and he succeeded, because the Pariement understood his position and was accommodating. The Universities had to be contented with the Jesuits' declaration that they did not share Santarelli's opinions and did not approve of them. In a conversation which was ostensibly friendly, but in which an unmistakably peremptory undertone was perceptible, he compelled Edmond Richer, the former syndic of the Sorbonne, and the author of the most violent work on the Gallican claims, to retract his opinions; but he also compelled the opposition party to recognize the independence of the State in temporal matters.

Meanwhile serious difficulties arose with England. To please the Pope and the Catholic party, as well as to appease his own conscience, certain secret promises in favour of the English Catholics had been inserted in the marriage contract of the French princess, which could not be laid before the English Parliament, and were not being realized. The English, who had hoped for alliance against Spain, were disappointed by the conclusion of peace. Queen Henrietta Maria and some of the priests who accompanied her had doubtless behaved imprudently; Charles I sent her French retinue back to France; the queen, whose marriage began with strife and bitterness, complained to the French Court; ambassadors came and went, but the relations between the two countries seemed only to become worse. Buckingham's personal resentment helped to aggravate the situation. In the war with Spain the English captured French ships which were conveying contraband goods to the Spanish Netherlands. War was declared.

Now Richelieu approached Spain, and a treaty of neutrality was concluded. The whole policy of France was suddenly given a different orientation. The ultramontane party was delighted: the party of "good Frenchmen" disappointed and exasperated. Canon Fancan, who had so zealously written in support of the Cardinal when Luynes was at the helm, and whom Richelieu had recently sent as diplomatic agent to Munich, now threatened to write against him, and fell a victim. With cold indifference Richelieu had his former collaborator sent to the Bastille as "an atheist, a friend of the Huguenots, a spy of the Lutherans." To him a human destiny, a human life, counted for nothing. Many, indeed, were those in Paris and the provinces, who, having somehow become dangerous to him, or having incurred his suspicion, disappeared behind the walls of some fortress and there died. To-day their very names are forgotten. Now and again the death of such a man in some keep or dungeon was indifferently announced in a letter.

The direction now assumed by French policy was not contrary to the main lines of Richelieu's policy; he had long intended to render the Huguenots innocuous; but now the difficulties were increased.

The backbone of the Huguenot power was La Rochelle. With its towers, bastions, and moats the city was at that time the most powerful sea-fortress in Europe, and was regarded as impregnable. In its narrow streets lived a strenuous, acquisitive, puritanical people of traders, who sent their fleets even to America. Here more than elsewhere a republican spirit prevailed; the city possessed extraordinary privileges and liberties; the mayor was elected yearly, and when he walked abroad a guard of bailiffs marched before him.

Not that Richelieu had desired civil war; but this bulwark of the opposition, this "wasps' nest," had to be reduced. In the immediate vicinity of the city, strongly fortified, eternally threatening it, and a standing cause of complaint, was Fort Saint-Louis, manned by a specially seasoned garrison, and commanded always by an officer in whom the king had the completest confidence; at present by M. de Toiras, who was one of the king's favourites, and whom Richelieu had for that reason very willingly sent out of Paris. Richelieu caused the Île de Ré and the Île d'Oléron, which lay opposite the city, to be fortified. In 1626 the Duc de Montmorency had been compelled, however unwillingly, to surrender his dignity of Admiral of France in return for a money indemnity; the old rank, which gave its holder almost unlimited power over all the coasts, harbours, and ships of France, was, like the rank of constable (abolished the year after old Lesdiguières died), no longer conferred; on the other hand, Richelieu had himself appointed grand master and intendant-general of the marine. He set to work feverishly,

RICHELIEU IN CAVALIER COSTUME
(*Copper-plate engraving by* Jérôme David. *Nationalbibliothek, Vienna*)

concerning himself with every detail of every ship; with the guns, ammunition, stores, flags, and signals; he succeeded in finding efficient collaborators, just as later he was able to find excellent seamen; and a fleet was created. "Nature herself," he says in his *Political Testament*, "has given France the lordship over the seas."

While Richelieu was pursuing the most cautious policy in respect of Spain, who was once more friendly, and avoiding a league against his former allies—Holland, Savoy, Venice, and the German Protestants—the whole "Protestant interest," as it was called in those days, threatened to turn against him. Buckingham sent Walter Montague, a son of the Earl of Manchester, on a secret mission to the Continent, which was to unite all these former allies—the German Protestants, Savoy, the Duke of Lorraine, and even the Emperor and Spain itself—in a league against France. The young Duke Charles IV was reigning in Nancy. Mme. de Chevreuse had fled to him as her husband's kinsman, and the young duke had immediately fallen in love with her. Montague arrived in Nancy, and the cold, elegant young Englishman was taken in the same net. For the Duchess, however, the love of these men was merely an instrument of revenge. No one could have been more active than she; she won over the Duke of Lorraine, who was the first to enter the league; she wrote to her friends in France; Montague dealt with the Duc de Rohan; and at Court the Comte de Soissons and the foolish young queen were in league with her. In those days, when even a great empire could put only a small army into the field, owing to the badness of the roads, the lack of *étapes*, and the difficulties of feeding the troops, the enmity of a small State like Lorraine might mean a great deal; moreover, the Kaiser was supposed to send an army to help the duke.

All these things were suspected in France, but no precise knowledge was available. Then Richelieu had Montague arrested on Spanish soil by French horse-troopers and conveyed to the Bastille. Never in her life—as she afterwards confessed—was Anne of Austria so alarmed. But Montague found an opportunity of letting her know that he had no papers with him which were compromising to her; on the other hand, Richelieu found proof of the great coalition which was forming against him. The English agent, since Richelieu had attained his end, was soon set at liberty.

But such a league, if indeed it came into being—and Montague's reports to his Court did not sound hopeful—and the necessary armaments, needed time for their completion. Richelieu reinforced the troops on the German and Flemish frontiers, and proceeded to his next task. The siege of La Rochelle is an epic. We have descriptions of it from so many of those who took part in it that we are acquainted with every detail of the operations. An army of 25,000 men lay before the city, under the command of the Duc d'Angoulême and the Maréchals Schomberg and Bassompierre; but the heart and soul of the besieging army and the real commander was Richelieu, who finally took the rank of a lieutenant-general. The discipline of the army was exceptional, for it was generously and punctually paid; the Cardinal and his collaborator, Père Joseph, saw that barracks and warm clothing and regular rations were provided. Père Joseph, for whom the war was a crusade, tried to enforce a religious discipline among the troops, and the camp was full of Capucin preachers. The king, who had a love of all things military, watched the naval actions and the storming parties, and even laid the guns; then he began to weary of the siege and went back to Paris, but returned again. Richelieu remained. The siege continued for a year. An exterior system of trenches invested the city, and a fleet of twenty-six warships blockaded the harbour; outside lay the English fleet; actions were fought for islands and forts; galleys and long-boats tried to break the blockade; fire-ships were driven against the enemy vessels; every attempt was made to gain the city, by hand-to-hand fighting, by negotiations, by treachery; a huge dam was built across the harbour, closing it in; the besieged, in their extremity, drove thousands of women, children, and men incapable of bearing arms out of the city; the soldiers stripped them of their clothes and drove them back, so that they perished miserably between the walls and the camp; but nevertheless the mayor, an obstinate seaman, would not listen to a word of surrender. At the same time letters were exchanged with all the courtesy of the seventeenth century. "You are not in a position to conduct peace negotiations with your ruler," wrote the Cardinal to the mayor and council of La Rochelle; "the mere thought is treasonable. But I beg you to believe that I fervently wish that you would give me cause to show my sympathy for you."

The first English fleet was defeated; on the 1st of May the beleaguered people saw the sails of a second fleet, but the admiral held that it was impossible to break the blockade, and turned home again. At Portsmouth Buckingham was murdered. Now all hope was destroyed. On the 29th of October, 1628, the king entered a city that was almost a city of the dead; only sixty-four Frenchmen and ninety Englishmen of the defenders were still capable of bearing arms.

The citizens were assured of their lives and the free exercise of their religion, but the city was deprived of all its privileges; the towers were pulled down, the walls levelled, the moats filled up, and a see of La Rochelle was established.

"The Synagogue of Satan is fallen," wrote the Pope in jubilation.

Throughout the south the war was continued, but when, on the 28th of June, 1629, peace was at last concluded, Richelieu showed that he had fought not a religious, but merely a political war: as a statesman, not as an ecclesiastic. As soon as the power of the king was re-established and acknowledged he received deputies and preachers in a friendly manner, and safeguarded everywhere their rights to the free exercise of their religion; and although in his heart he was all for their conversion and for unity of faith, he strove to curb the zeal of the Catholic party and the fanatical priests. Under him, as under Mazarin, the French Protestants became the most loyal supporters of the monarchy.

LA ROCHELLE

Those who had helped him to overthrow the enemy within the gates had a foreboding of what had happened and of what must follow. "So we shall be stupid enough to conquer La Rochelle," was Bassompierre's intelligent remark. The majority of the French magnates had not believed that the city would be taken; they had hoped that the Cardinal would founder on this rock.

The death of Buckingham, the defeat of the English fleet, and the fall of La Rochelle had already led to peace with England: it was concluded on the 24th of April, 1629. In vain had Rohan and the synod of Nîmes reminded the king of his promises. England wished to have a free hand in Germany, and had no desire to burden herself any longer with a hopeless task. On the other hand, Richelieu for his part refused to intercede for the English Catholics. What a part personality may play is shown by the fact that the English Court stipulated for a pardon for Mme. de Chevreuse as a condition of the peace, and that Richelieu, so that he should not be forced to agree, had already allowed her to return to France. "She ought to give the queen another opportunity of having a child," said the Duc d'Orléans scornfully.

CHAPTER X

THE CRISIS

DURING the siege of La Rochelle a fresh cause of dispute with Spain had arisen. In the matter of external politics the differences between France and Spain were too great; and although Spain had at times, on religious grounds, given a lukewarm assistance against the Huguenots, she had, from political motives, quite as frequently supported them. When he was left in the lurch by England, Rohan had turned to the Spaniards, and they had concluded an alliance with him. Philip IV pointed to the precedent that France had supported his rebellious subjects in the Netherlands. In Mantua the last duke of the reigning house of Gonzaga had died, and Charles de Nevers, of the French branch of that house, was his heir in Mantua and Montferrat. The Spaniards did not wish to see a French ruler in either of these provinces, which bordered on the eastern and western frontiers of the duchy of Milan, and in which lay the strongest fortresses in Upper Italy—Mantua and Casale. They favoured a candidate of the Guastalla family. The Emperor was appealed to as feudal lord. The covetous, resolute old Charles Emmanuel of Savoy laid claim to the inheritance of Montferrat and came to an agreement with the Spaniards. In February 1628 the marquisate was invaded by a Spanish army on one side and a Piedmontese force on the other, and the Spaniards, under Gonzalvo de Cordoba, besieged Casale.

Richelieu was willing neither to leave the French princes in the lurch, nor to permit enemy powers to gain possession of the two fortresses. At first he tried negotiations; but as soon as La Rochelle had fallen, in the autumn of 1628, a French army, marching through snow and ice, crossed the Alps in winter, and in March stormed the pass of Susa and compelled Charles Emmanuel, sorely against his will, to renew the alliance with France and to renounce Montserrat. The Spaniards were forced to raise the siege of Casale. Richelieu left a force in Italy, with Toiras as commandant in Casale; he himself remained in Susa, while the king continued the war against the Protestants.

To Spain, the "world Power," as to the Emperor, it seemed intolerable that France should decide an Italian question. The Spaniards sent Spinola to Milan, and the Emperor decided to send Wallenstein into Italy. For the time being Collalto came in his place.

The great war, which for ten years had been devastating Germany, threatened to become a European war. Richelieu wished by all means to avert this. His policy was a defensive one; he was endeavouring to free France from her encirclement, and to prevent Spain from becoming still more powerful and dangerous. During these years endless negotiations were conducted in all directions. Richelieu states in his *Political Testament* that it was not until five or six years after he had first come into power that he realized how useful it is to negotiate perpetually over everything. To his policy, which was based on a network of profoundly complicated threads, a constant balancing of all the forces involved, and a whole system of reinsurance—a policy which only a man of his intellectual power and ingenuity could have prosecuted—negotiation was essential. Merely to combine the politically important religious interests with the interests of the nation represented an almost insoluble problem. To avoid losing the Protestant Leaguers, who were indispensable against the Habsburgs, and yet to retain the friendship of the Catholic powers, and to achieve peace without losing the advantage! Even in the very midst of the great war there was a good deal of earnest and fantastic talk of a world peace. Not only had Carlo Gonzaga sought to unite the Christian world in a crusade against the Turks; in 1619, together with a Count Althann, he had founded an order of Christian militia in Vienna, which was blessed by the Pope and derided by the Parisians; he had received ambassadors from all the Balkan countries, who promised a common insurrection and an expedition against Constantinople; he had visited the Courts of Middle and Eastern Europe, and had sought to unite France with the Emperor and Spain. On account of the ever-threatening Turkish peril, and the severely religious life of the period, these plans were taken more seriously than seems justified to-day—and yet not altogether seriously. In all ages comprehensive ideas, hopes, and purposes have floated in the air, occupying men's minds and on all men's lips; always to be shattered by the more immediate and imperious

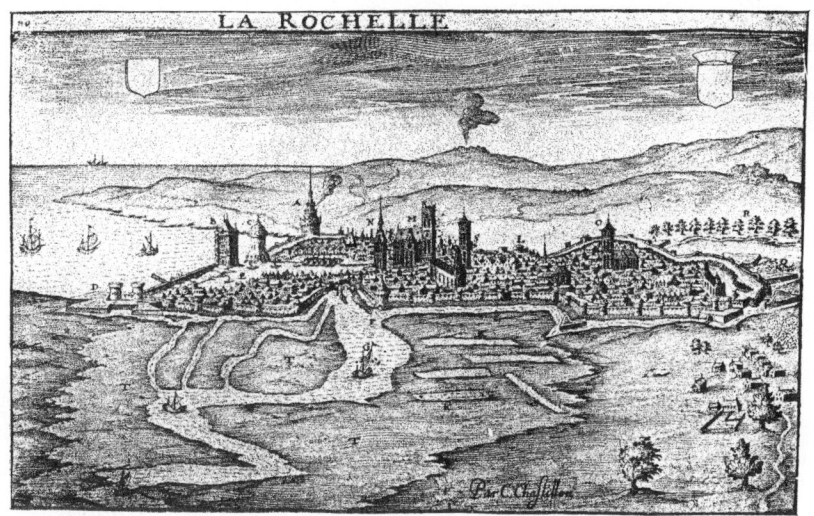

LA ROCHELLE
(*From* "*Topographie française.*" Claude Chastillon, *Paris*, 1641)

A COMPANY
(*Drawing by* Jacques Callot, *engraved by* Israel. *From* "*Les Misères et les Malheurs de la Guerre*," *Paris*, 1633. *Albertina, Vienna*)

problems of interest and prestige—of "reputation," as it was called in Richelieu's time.

In order to avert the threatened war in Upper Italy, the Pope sent an embassy to which an able young Papal officer, Giulio Mazarini, was attached. He rode to and fro, negotiating with Spinola, who once more lay before Casale, with the Imperial Commander, Collalto, who was besieging Mantua, with Charles Emmanuel, in Turin, and with Richelieu, who had recently crossed the Alps.

Charles Emmanuel of Savoy had already formed a secret alliance with Spain, and in urgent letters was entreating the Emperor to give Wallenstein the order to invade France. But Richelieu, whom no protestations and no threats could divert from his purpose, who was not to be deceived, and was himself impenetrable, was moving downwards with his army in order to relieve Casale. He had no provisions for his 34,000 men, for Savoy refused to supply them, and if he advanced any farther he would have the Piedmontese army at his back and the Spanish and Austrian armies before him. At the last parleys he had appeared gloomy and thoughtful. His enemies held him for lost. But in pursuance of a plan which he had formed some time previously he made a feint against Turin, moved in forced marches in a south-westerly direction, and stormed the Savoyard fortress of Pinerolo, which opened up the shortest line of communication with France and gave him not only security but the most advantageous position.

This was in March 1630. In August a new French army defeated the Piedmontese at Avigliana;

but Mantua was taken and laid waste by the Austrians, and still war was not declared. Peace negotiations were proceeding in Madrid as in Italy, while at the seat of war each side was endeavouring to secure the advantage. Spinola was pushing forward his field fortifications towards the valiantly defended Casale, while Richelieu was hoping to relieve it. "All Europe was now watching Casale," as before it had watched La Rochelle.

Meanwhile the Emperor had convoked the Reichstag at Regensburg. Ferdinand II saw all his adversaries defeated; he had promulgated the Edict of Restitution and had in great measure carried it out; the Imperial power was now at its height, though it was soon to be in a very different position. Wallenstein wished to increase the strength of his army to 150,000. Ferdinand's son, the king of Hungary, was to be elected king of Rome in the Reichstag. The Estates, and even the Catholic princes, regarded the Imperial power with anxiety; the Pope feared it, so that the tightly strung bow threatened to break. As yet the Emperor had no foreboding of danger, but he met with unexpected and unwelcome opposition; he found the electoral princes by no means eager to elect his son, and all, Protestants and Catholics alike, were opposed to Wallenstein and his plans. There was a general desire for peace and disarmament. All the Catholic Powers, and of the Protestant Powers England, and even Richelieu himself, had sent embassies to Regensburg—with various intentions. What Richelieu desired in Germany was what he called a "true peace," a "balance" between the Emperor and

THE CRISIS

the princes, to maintain which the princes would need the help of France, while the Empire would be powerless abroad. While the Protestant allies were indispensable to him, Catholic allies would have been much more welcome, and he had already made repeated attempts to win Bavaria and the League for France—attempts which had hitherto been fruitless. In this direction, too, an advantage might perhaps be secured in respect of the solution of the Italian question.

On July 2, 1630, Père Joseph left him in Grenoble; he was to accompany the actual ambassador, the Prior of Léon, Charles Brûlart, as the Cardinal's confidential agent. In Memmingen they encountered Wallenstein, with whom Père Joseph held lengthy conversations—both of them, the monk and the general, men of action with a touch of the visionary, though the monk was more of an enthusiast than the soldier. They spoke of the conquest of Constantinople, the final goal of their desires; and Wallenstein seems on this occasion to have made some very remarkable statements in relation to his plans. On August 2nd the envoys had their first audience of the Emperor in Regensburg, in the presence of Father Lamormaini; they had already dispatched couriers to ask for fresh powers, but by the time they returned the events and the negotiations had outstripped them. On August 22nd Chavigny, who had accompanied them, was sent to the Cardinal to make a verbal report; he found him on September 2nd in Lyons, and received fresh instructions on the 3rd and 4th, which by the 19th were in the hands of the envoys. We must reflect upon the distances to be covered and the difficulties of travel in those days in order to realize the delays and impediments that occurred during all negotiations and the time which these occupied. So many problems had now to be considered in connection with the Italian question alone; the episcopal sees, the enfeoffment of Charles Gonzaga, indemnities, errors in calculation, provinces, pledges of security, and rights of garrison; but the Imperial commissioners —the Abbot Anton von Kremsmünster and the Herren von Nostitz and von Questenberg—gave precedence to the discussion of the general peace. The Emperor was honestly anxious for peace with Catholic France. It was represented to the envoys that Richelieu had in the meantime approached Sweden; that Gustavus Adolphus, who was already on German soil, had spoken in the name of a Protestant French alliance, and guarantees were demanded against such an alliance. As yet no alliance existed; but when Chavigny reached Richelieu with these demands the latter at once recognized that he must get free of Sweden, which was at war with the Emperor—while he could not demand that the Emperor should break with Spain, because there was officially no war between France and Spain.

Everything was thus undecided, and the envoys, while they continued their negotiations—and not only with the Emperor, but in many directions—were uncertain of their ground. And suddenly they ceased to receive instructions.

Richelieu found himself hemmed in. The most serious crisis of his Government had arisen. It had long been prepared. Marie de' Medici, who had made him minister, expected and demanded that he should serve her before all. He had promised to do so; but he had silently taken it for granted that she would follow his advice, and that the political necessities of the realm, as he saw them and expounded them, would take precedence of all else. But this was not the queen-mother's view of the matter. She was affronted and enraged when he did not comply with her desires and caprices. She had already been greatly annoyed when he required the king's presence before La Rochelle, at a time when she wanted her son beside her in Paris. Moreover, she had been unwilling for the king to accompany the army into Italy, because of her dislike of Charles de Nevers. Meanwhile Gaston d'Orléans, whose first wife—so forcibly wedded to him—had died in child-bed, had fallen in love with the Princess Maria di Gonzaga, the daughter of the duke, and wished at all costs to marry her. Doubly exasperated, the queen had wished to banish the princess from the Court, had then had her imprisoned, and finally, moved by her son's entreaties, had suddenly restored her to liberty. When he at last renounced the princess she demanded, as his reward, the governorships of the provinces of Burgundy and Champagne. Of this unthinkable and unthinking policy, which was inspired merely by a mother's anger and a mother's love, Richelieu would hear nothing. Never would he entrust the frontier provinces and their fortresses to the frivolous, senseless, and disloyal Orléans.

On January 13, 1629, he had presented her and

the king with a review of the European situation and an abstract of his plans for the future, which constituted a grandiose and expansive programme; he worked with her as of old, and initiated her in everything, in the hope that she would understand and co-operate with him. The passionate, foolish woman had no such intention; she could only see that the man whom she had made what he was would not do as she desired. And since he was no longer continually at her side he had no longer the same influence over her. She was now entirely in the hands of the ultramontane party, which was discontented with Richelieu, disapproved of the dispute with Spain, and took advantage of Marie de' Medici's feminine tantrums to incite her against the Cardinal. In the keeper of the Seal, Marillac, he had an opponent in the Cabinet itself.

In May 1629 Richelieu stated, for the first time, in a letter to the young Queen Anne, that he had heard that the queen-mother's feelings towards him had altered. He wrote to her still with extreme courtesy and with assurances of his devotion; but she was furious, and when in the autumn Gaston left France on the pretext that he no longer felt safe there, she treated the Cardinal with such obvious displeasure that on September 14th he submitted his resignation. The king shed bitter tears; but he did not accept the resignation. He brought about a reconciliation, and two months later, on November 21, 1629, Richelieu was appointed "chief minister of the State." The Duc d'Orléans was induced to return by large presents of money and other governorships.

But the queen-mother was reconciled only in appearance; she and her younger son had promised one another, in writing, to overthrow Richelieu; they had given the document, which was enclosed in a golden capsule, into the keeping of the old Duc de Bellegarde, who wore it on a golden chain round his neck. When the king, whose health had long been shattered by a chronic bowel complaint, fell seriously ill in Lyons (this was during the Savoy campaign, and while negotiations were proceeding in Regensburg), he was tenderly nursed by his mother and his wife, but both women took advantage of the opportunity to speak against the Cardinal. By the end of September the king lay apparently dying; the women, thirsting for revenge, extracted a promise from the exhausted man that he would dismiss the Cardinal as soon as the war was ended and the peace with Spain concluded.

In the beginning, despite his anxieties, Richelieu had remained with the army, and only at the end of August, when the plague broke out in Italy, did he proceed to Lyons. One can imagine what a life he led in those days. He himself was always ailing; the fate of a campaign, extensive plans for the future, the problem of a European war, and the negotiations which might, and indeed must, avert its outbreak—endless and difficult deliberations respecting the most intricate transactions in the remote distance—all these things were weighing upon him; and now that the king was so seriously ill he could not be sure that the morrow would see him still a minister, or that on the king's death he would not lose his liberty and his life. All those who had power at Court, and those who were then coming into power, were his deadly enemies; how many of those who now represented themselves to be his friends would be left to him, and what could those who were really his friends do for him when the king was dead? Unshaken, he persisted on his way; indefatigably he continued his labours; but we can understand why the envoys in Regensburg did not receive their instructions in time.

And since they had received no fresh instructions, and had learned of the king's previous illness, they believed themselves justified in exceeding their original instructions; and on the morning of October 13, 1630, they concluded a treaty of peace and alliance which was more or less in accordance with the desires of the Emperor Ferdinand. Not until five days later, on October 18th, did Richelieu's dispatches come to hand—dispatches conceived in a very different spirit.

The king recovered. But the queen-mother had his promise, and when, on the 20th, the news of the peace reached Lyons, she had rockets sent up from the courtyard of the château; rejoicing—as she expressly told the Princess de Conti—not so much over the peace, as because the minister whom she now hated so bitterly, because she had formerly loved him, was to suffer downfall.

"The treaty is invalid," wrote Richelieu in a brief memorandum on October 21st, "because M. de Léon has exceeded his authority. He was to negotiate only for the peace in Italy; he had no authority to conclude a treaty of alliance between the Emperor and France." Then a brief allusion is made to some other inadmissible agreements which "France to all appearances would have to concede to the allies." He had the more cause to oppose the treaty of peace in that the situation of France at the seat of war had become very much more favourable; and he forthwith undeceived the French generals. Schomberg, who was commanding for him in Italy, had already, on his own responsibility, declared that such a peace was impossible, and, ignoring the treaty, had crossed the Po with 22,000 men and taken up his position before Casale—a step which had Richelieu's entire approval. A battle would have ensued had not the adroitness and ambition of the young Mazarini negotiated a treaty between the two fronts—although the artillery had already opened fire, and Ottavio Piccolomini had had his horse shot under him—by which Casale was provisionally surrendered to Gonzaga, and received a French garrison, while an Imperial commissary took over the administration pending a final settlement.

All the important fortresses on the eastern frontiers of Italy—Susa, Pinerolo, and Casale—were for the time being in French hands, and the war with Spain was averted.

Richelieu accompanied the queen-mother to Paris, and did his best to win her, as of old, by the utmost assiduity and affability. Marie de' Medici was no whit less amiable. But hardly had she arrived in Paris when she dismissed Mme. de Combalet, Richelieu's niece, who had hitherto been her lady-in-waiting, and with her every servant and officer whom she had ever taken into her service on Richelieu's recommendation. On November 10th that famous understanding was arrived at which has made this day known to history as the "Day of Dupes."

The course of events is described in various records with variations of detail; every observer naturally heard and saw what occurred in his own fashion; but so much may be stated with certainty: On November 9th the king had tried to effect a reconciliation between his brother and the Cardinal, and Monsieur, with visible reluctance, coldly and unamiably, had accepted the Cardinal's explanations. On the morning of the 10th Louis XIII sought his mother in the Luxembourg; she and the king shut themselves up in her study, and no one was permitted to enter. Richelieu, who suspected what was afoot, and who likewise drove up to the queen's palace, found all the doors closed. But he knew and took a way into the queen's cabinet which led through the private chapel. Smiling, he entered the room—one can imagine the smile on that narrow face, with its little, pointed beard—entered with the words: "I would wager that Your Majesties are speaking of me." Thereupon the queen lost control of herself, giving full expression to her passionate hatred. Richelieu sank to his knees and asked what he had done, assured her of his loyalty, begged for her forgiveness if he had offended her, wept and entreated, but all in vain. She raved on, appealing to the king's promise, and Richelieu left the palace in despair.

It seems that Père Joseph and others attempted to make peace, but without success. The king, for whom speech was never easy, and who apparently was incapable of withstanding his mother's wrath, left

Paris in a state of agitation and despondency, and drove to Versailles, where he had a small hunting-box. The grand master of the horse, the Marquis de Saint-Simon, the father of the historian, and Cardinal de la Valette, spoke in Richelieu's favour. Richelieu himself believed that he was lost, and was already anxious to leave Paris. Bassompierre, who was to have dined with him that day, heard that he was leaving, and was surprised when the Cardinal said to him: "You will no longer rate very highly one like myself, from whom everything has been taken." The Maréchal supposed that Richelieu was thinking of Monsieur's unfriendly behaviour of the previous day. Later, while he was dining with the Duc de Créqui, he learned that the Cardinal was dismissed. Thereupon, it seems, he had a great deal to say of the matter, which subsequently proved to be very unfortunate for him. For in the meanwhile the king had sent for Richelieu; the Cardinal drove to Versailles and threw himself at the king's feet; whereupon the king bade him stand up, assured him of his favour, and spoke further with him in private.

In the evening there was a thronged and festive gathering in the Luxembourg; the whole Court did homage to the old queen. On the following morning it was learned that the Cardinal was still first minister, while the keeper of the Seal, De Marillac, the queen-mother's confidant in the ministry, was dismissed and banished from the Court. Promptly the rooms of the Luxembourg emptied themselves, and all flocked to the house of the Cardinal. Châteauneuf was appointed keeper of the Seal in Marillac's place.

Richelieu was victorious; and it had been one of the most difficult victories of his career. He had done with the queen whom he had served so long. He saw clear before him the narrow path which he must tread.

But the woman was blind to all but the goal of her passion. She repulsed all attempts at negotiation; she declined to appear in the council; she refused to hear of a reconciliation, and in her obstinate anger she continued to make fresh difficulties, until at last she was forbidden to remain in Paris and was banished to the provinces.

And so that came to pass which to the world appeared monstrous; which agitated the Court, and France, and all Europe, and let loose a flood of polemical writings, a torrent of savage wrath, of violent attacks and calumnies, and endless abuse against the minister; the queen-mother, after various fruitless attempts to promote rebellion and dictate her conditions as of old, was forced to leave the country, and fled to the Infanta Clara Eugenia, the wife of the Spanish viceroy in Brussels. A last attempt at reconciliation, which Père Joseph had wished to undertake, fell through, as the latter had injured his foot and was unable to travel. Her younger son followed her example. Continually inflamed by his mother, and by foolish and ambitious members of his household, always suffering from a grievance and full of crazy pretensions, he too at last fled the country, taking refuge first in Lorraine and then in Brussels.

Against him as the heir to the throne no proceedings were taken. But all his adherents were declared guilty of *lèse-majesté*—which was equivalent to the modern offence of high treason. The Parlement, which was already strenuously opposing the autocratic will of the minister, refused by an equality of votes to register the decree. The king summoned the Parlement to the Louvre, and informed it that it had the right of speech, but not the right of intervention in affairs of State; and a number of presidents and councillors were banished.

Even before this the Duchess d'Elbœuf, the widow of the Connétable de Lesdiguières, and other ladies of the Court, were banished. Bassompierre, the admired pattern of all young noblemen, the darling of the ladies, was arrested on February 25, 1631, by a lieutenant of the bodyguard, who apologized in tears for arresting him, and was taken to the Bastille. He had been warned, and when he saw that the king no longer spoke to him, but turned his head away, he had realized what was in store for him, and on the day before his imprisonment he had burned six thousand love-letters. He was the lover of the Princess de Conti, among other ladies, and she had borne him a son. She had been of the queen-mother's party, and he must have compromised himself by his affection for her. " Bassompierre is doing penance for his evil tongue," wrote Richelieu. He sent Bassompierre a rosary, and wrote, with a touch of that humour which by no means befitted the dismal occasion and in which he betrayed the utter coldness of his heart, that the Maréchal might now seek favour of his Creator, as he had formerly sought it of His creatures. The Princess de Conti was banished to Eu, and died on April 30th of "this year of misfortune." Bassompierre spent twelve years in the Bastille; when he came out of it after Richelieu's death he was an old man. Richelieu wrote to the king: "I shall cut so short the claws of all those of whom we should beware that all their wicked intentions will be unavailing."

The queen's physician, Vautier, was sent to prison; the king's confessor, Père Suffren, who spoke in her favour, was dismissed. The brother of the keeper of the Seal, the Maréchal de Marillac, a handsome and stately man, who, like his brother, had risen from a humble position by the queen's favour, had already been arrested in Italy (on November 21st), and was brought before a special tribunal at Verdun, on a charge of extortion and embezzlement. His trial was long protracted, the Court was dissolved, the marshal was sent from one prison to another, and at last, in 1632, was taken to Richelieu's château at Ruel, not far from Paris. There a new special tribunal was constituted of three-and-twenty selected judges, under the presidency of Châteauneuf, the new Minister of Justice, which after twelve hours' deliberation sentenced the prisoner to death by a majority of one. Marie de' Medici and Monsieur had written to the judges that they would have to answer with their lives and property for what was done to the Maréchal. On the following day he was taken to Paris and beheaded. The Parlement had protested in vain. Richelieu, who in his harshest and most cold-blooded transactions was fond of playing the part of a disinterested observer, is reported to have said: "He must have been guilty, since the judges have so decided"—a curiously solemn comedy, which deceived no one, least of all his confidants.

The waves of this revolution in the Royal house bore away many a victim. The Duc de Guise, who was summoned to Paris to justify himself, relinquished his governorship of Provence, took ship for Italy, and did not return. But there was one victim who above all others drew the gaze of the world—the Duc de Montmorency. This godchild of Henri IV was one of those happy beings who give happiness wherever they go and are beloved by all. No genius, but handsome, valiant, knightly, generous, delightful to look at, and charming and lovable by nature, he was the idol of the soldiery and the people. A victor in the naval battle of the islands off La Rochelle, a victor in the hills of Avigliana, he did not feel that he was rewarded and esteemed beyond his deserts. A distant kinsman, the Comte de Montmorency-Boutteville, had been executed on account of a duel. Richelieu had induced the duke to surrender his office as Admiral of France, and had, it seems, if somewhat ambiguously, led him to expect the appointment of field-marshal-general; but the Cardinal did not care to see the great nobles rise too high. Montmorency was already marshal of France and governor of Languedoc. There were lesser causes of mortification; moreover, his vassals and his acquaintances incited him to protest, and when the Duc d'Orléans sent him word that he was marching on France with an army, in alliance with Charles IV of Lorraine, the imprudent and embittered man allowed himself to be led away.

When, on June 11, 1632, Gaston crossed the frontier, making boastful proclamations, Montmorency went to meet him. He came with only a small troop, for the provinces had not, as he expected, risen against the Cardinal, and he met a wretched army of a few regiments, which were already cut off from their base by Schomberg and La Force. A French army had entered Lorraine before the duke could make a move. Before Castelnaudary they were completely defeated. Montmorency, after breaking through the enemy's ranks, was made a prisoner, suffering from seven severe wounds. When half convalescent he was taken to Toulouse, and was there brought before a commission of the Parlement, once more presided over by Châteauneuf, on a charge of high treason. He encountered his judges with knightly courtesy, confessing himself guilty; it was true, he said, that as a peer of France he might have refused to recognize that court, but his crime was of such a nature that he placed himself absolutely at His Majesty's disposal. All marvelled at his self-control. Only once was it broken, when Châteauneuf asked his name: "You have eaten the bread of our house long enough to know it," he replied. All Toulouse, and indeed all France, waited in grief and anxiety. Charles I of England, the Venetian Republic, and the Duke of Savoy sent envoys to plead for his pardon; the whole nobility of France was roused; the Cardinal la Valette, for whom Richelieu had a special affection, had the sacrament exposed in all the churches of his diocese, and appointed prayers. Montmorency's young wife, Felicia Orsini, had hastened to Toulouse, but no one

THE MARÉCHAL DE BASSOMPIERRE
(Painter unknown. Versailles)

THE DUC DE MONTMORENCY
(Copper-plate engraving by Mariette. Nationalbibliothek, Vienna)

would receive her. His sister, the beautiful Princess de Condé, threw herself at Richelieu's feet; he, too, kneeled, and assured her that he could do nothing. Officers and nobles implored the king to be merciful. Louis XIII took refuge in gloomy silence. "I have not the right," he said, "to entertain the feelings of a private person."

Montmorency made his will, in which he gave to his friends a last proof of his courtesy and affection. To Richelieu he bequeathed a picture from his collections; an instance of the highest courtesy in face of death which was in accordance with the manners of the age, which valued courtesy and deportment and "form" above all things. He had to comfort and encourage his confessor; he had never gone into action more calmly than he went to the block. On August 30, 1632, his head fell in the inner courtyard of the Capitol of Toulouse.

His despairing wife retired to a convent. His sister and her family reserved their revenge on Châteauneuf for a later day. Worst of all behaved the members of the Royal family. Gaston d'Orléans once more forsook and betrayed all his adherents in order to make peace with the Court. The Prince of Condé had eyes for one thing only—the great Montmorency inheritance; he received the sequestrated properties of his executed brother-in-law. It was then that Enghien and Chantilly passed to the house of Condé. Four days after the execution, in an address with which he opened the session of the Estates of the province of Burgundy, the prince proclaimed the depth of his gratitude and obligation to the Cardinal. He wrote complaining letters to the widow in her convent because he had found that certain individual articles were missing which formed part of the dead man's estate and were therefore his property.

All France had shuddered when the head of the first baron of the realm fell upon the scaffold. Men were not accustomed to seeing great nobles punished for rebellion. The civil war seemed, in a sense, to justify them. The execution of Montmorency was the tragic symbol of the declining authority of the nobles and the terrible power of Richelieu.

The people found no cause to rejoice in the change. That in the meantime, by the treaty of Cherasco, negotiated by the cunning of the young Mazarini, the fortress of Pinerolo, the key to Upper Italy, was at last surrendered to France; that Savoy under its new ruler, Duke Victor Amadeus, had come permanently under French influence; that in Germany, by the Treaty of Fontainebleau, the interests of Bavaria were allied with those of France; that through Richelieu's masterly statecraft the position of France in Europe had been raised to such a height as it had never before attained; that in the interior a limit had been set to disorder and insubordination—of all this the people were oblivious. They were conscious only of the burden of armaments and of the increase of taxation; they saw the special tribunals and their sanguinary judgments, which were contrary to their sense of justice, their privileges and traditions;

they saw that great priest ruling the country for whom the king had driven his own mother from him, and from whom an exhalation of bloodshed and terror was beginning to spread through the land.

CHAPTER XI

RICHELIEU'S WAR POLICY

At Regensburg the Emperor had not attained his desire. The king of Hungary was not elected king of the Romans. Wallenstein, his dangerous instrument, he had been forced to sacrifice to the princes, who were still united against him; the ideal of making the Imperial power a reality within the empire had not been achieved. The French policy, as represented by Père Joseph, had to this failure added its own. "The Capucin has six elector's hats hidden in his hood," Ferdinand is said to have remarked. There was great bitterness of feeling between Maximilian of Bavaria and the Emperor.

But all the French hopes and plans which had been founded on this momentary state of equilibrium in Germany were overthrown by the rapid advance of Gustavus Adolphus. France had herself brought this dangerous ally on the scene by negotiating a peace between Sweden and Poland. Gustavus Adolphus, before he began his campaign, had sent envoys to all the Powers which were opposed to the Emperor—to France, Venice, and the States-General of the Netherlands. For Père Joseph, Sweden was a poison that had to be employed as an antidote; if the Habsburg were sufficiently weakened by Sweden, France should and would be the foremost Catholic Power. In January 1631, after protracted negotiations, the treaty of

Bärwald was concluded, according to which France was to pay a subsidy to Sweden. This was the time of the so-called "covert war" against the Habsburg power; the payment of subsidies, according to the international law of those days, did not constitute an act of war. But Gustavus Adolphus was victorious too quickly, and not as France had intended. Instead of marching on Vienna he turned on the Catholic princes of South Germany, without troubling about their "neutrality," which had been the subject of an agreement with France. Quite naturally Maximilian of Bavaria, himself injured and threatened, and impelled by his religious feelings, went over once more to the Emperor. To Richelieu's great consternation, the Swedes appeared on the left bank of the Rhine, on the French frontier, in which position they were, to his thinking, by no means desirable neighbours. Gustavus Adolphus, however, challenged France to form an offensive alliance; then he could take the left bank of the Rhine and the Franche Comté of Burgundy. To the majority of the French councillors the plan seemed an attractive one. Père Joseph spoke vehemently against it, and after a sleepless night Richelieu admitted that he was in the right. Gustavus Adolphus's conquests were too extensive; one could not pursue the anti-Catholic policy so far; moreover, there were only 15,000 men available on the eastern frontier. . . . The Cardinal continued his negotiations; but he had to look on while in the course of the year (1632) Sweden took possession of almost the whole of Alsace.

Then, at the battle of Lützen, Gustavus Adolphus

fell. The majority of his allies were conscious of a sense of liberation, while the Pope, instead of the expected *Te Deum*, celebrated a silent mass. The Swedish king had founded a Duchy of Franconia, and had received the homage of its feudatories; and as a condition of peace he had stipulated to the Emperor that he, Gustavus Adolphus, should be King of the Romans. A great Swedish-North-German empire, as the result of the French policy, would have been a bitter pill to swallow. However, the death of the Swede once more averted the danger which in those years Richelieu feared above all things, that the Emperor might turn against France.

In 1629 Richelieu had expounded his foreign policy to the king : France must build up a sea power, turn Metz into a very strong fortress (that was due to the three bishoprics which since the middle of the sixteenth century had actually been in the power of France), and obtain a thoroughfare to Italy through Savoy—which had now been secured by the capture of Pinerolo; it was possible by peaceful means to obtain Neufchâtel from the Duc de Longueville, and, if it came to war with Spain, to acquire Navarre and the Franche Comté of Burgundy; and one might consider making a thrust at Strasburg in order to secure "a door into Germany."

Since then the situation had been completely transformed, and all Richelieu's plans were developed out of this situation, for he never laid down a theoretical policy.

Sweden must be driven back. But the Swedish army, the Swedish generals, were needed to oppose the Emperor. One must keep in with them and the Protestant princes, and yet at the same time spare the feelings of the Catholics, and everywhere maintain the Catholic worship—"Only, no religious war!" said Père Joseph—and thus make sure of the neutrality of the Catholic princes, so that they would not combine with the Emperor. If all this could be achieved, and if the war was successful, there was a hope of confining the Emperor to his heritage; he would lose even Hungary and Bohemia. The war aims of France were, the final and legal possession of the three bishoprics of Metz, Toul, and Verdun, and of Lorraine, with whom France was at war. Apart from this, no territorial conquests were desired. It was important for France that no separate or partial peace should be concluded, through which she might be isolated, but only a general peace. This was Richelieu's principle to the last. And since he was disquieted by the danger of a separate peace between Holland and Spain, he sent Charnacé, one of his ablest diplomatists, who had already conducted the very important negotiations with Gustavus Adolphus, to Holland, and proposed the partition of the Spanish Netherlands. To Germany, when Sweden and the Protestant Estates of West Germany had unanimously combined in the League of Heilbronn, he sent the Marquis de Feuquières, a cousin of Père Joseph's. France demanded that the left bank of the Rhine, and above all the fortress of Philippsburg, should be surrendered as security for her war aims. The attempts at negotiation were numerous and protracted; on every hand there were difficulties, not the least of which was jealousy;

finally, in 1633, a treaty was concluded at Heilbronn with Sweden, and in September with the Protestants.

At this juncture Count Kinsky, sent by Wallenstein, appeared in company with Feuquières. In Paris a special session of the cabinet was held for the purpose of considering Wallenstein's proposals. He was offered money, the prospect of the Bohemian crown, a diversion in his favour. This was in May; after the famous declaration of the forty-two colonels on January 12, 1634, the matter was taken more seriously, and M. de La Boderie was sent to him; but on February 25th Wallenstein was murdered in Eger.

Negotiations were opened with Oxenstjerna, who, for a million livres, was willing to evacuate all Germany as far as the Elbe; in which proposal Richelieu saw no advantage whatever for France. Then once again the whole situation was transformed by the heavy defeat suffered by Horn and Bernhard von Weimar at Nördlingen, on September 6, 1634, at the hands of the Imperial General Gallas. At the news of this disaster Richelieu, who was at Monceau with the king, returned with all possible haste to Paris; the aggressive war against France, which he so greatly feared, might at any moment become a reality. Now the two parties came far towards meeting one another; the Swedish envoy Leffler made large offers, and Richelieu was prepared openly to participate in the war; a French army of 12,000 men was to cross the Rhine; a second army would be stationed on the left bank. Since the Swedes could no longer hold out in Alsace, French troops had already occupied the Alsatian cities. Richelieu demanded that Alsace, with the fortress of Breisach—which was not yet taken—should be given to him as security until the conclusion of peace; and since France was now putting armies into the field she would pay no more subsidies, and would take an equal part in the conduct of the campaign. To these conditions the Swedish chancellor, Oxenstjerna, refused to agree. He first sent the Dutchman, Hugo Grotius, the scholar and statesman, to Compiègne, and then followed himself. Richelieu found Grotius stiff and Oxenstjerna "truly Gothic"; but fresh victories and advances on the part of the Imperial armies were forcing a conclusion, and on April 15, 1635, it was resolved in council that having so long fought the Habsburg power in a covert fashion, France would now openly take part in the war.

No one was better pleased than Louis XIII. He loved war, and Richelieu celebrated its opening with ballets and festivities. On the other hand, the Catholic party was greatly irritated and embittered by the alliance with the Protestants. Agreement had already been reached with Holland on February 8th. France was counting on a conspiracy against the Spanish rule in Belgium, and was hoping to bring about a general alliance of the Italian States against Spain. But the Signoria of Venice cautiously held back, and in Rome the Spanish influence was once again the more powerful, and the policy of Urban VIII had undergone a change; only Savoy joined France—because she had to—and Mantua. England remained neutral because the lucrative sea-borne trade between Flanders and Spain was more important to her than the restoration of the Palatinate.

On May 19, 1635, the herald, Jehan Gratiollet, preceded by the royal trumpeter Gratien Elissavide, rode up to the gates of Brussels and requested an audience of the viceroy, the Cardinal-Infante Don Fernando. The burgomaster, accompanied by the herald of the Golden Fleece, refused at first to admit him; then he was put off, and the audience was not granted. The herald waited until the evening in the midst of a thronging crowd; then he threw the declaration of war across the Place, and while two Spanish heralds cried that no one was to pick it up, Jehan Gratiollet, with his trumpeter, spurred his horse through the mob and away; at the frontier he had a parley blown, and fastened the declaration to a post.

In Paris the *Gazette de France* published a manifesto composed by Père Joseph. War had been declared only on Spain, and the reason assigned for the war was the fact that the Spaniards had captured and taken to Brussels the Elector of Trier, Johan Philipp von Sötern, who, out of fear of the Swedes, had placed himself under French protection. This diplomatic caution had not much point; the Imperial troops were fighting against the French no less than the Spanish army. On May 30, 1635, a fortnight after the French declaration of war, the peace of Prague was concluded, in which the majority of the Protestant princes united in joining the Emperor.

France had placed four armies in the field; on paper she had 135,000 foot and 21,000 cavalry; a very great force for those days, but it was never at its full strength. A hundred new regiments had been improvised of foreign soldiers—Swiss, German, Irish, and, later on, Polish; for with the French there was little to be done, as Richelieu was for ever complaining. Extremely valiant, and almost irresistible in battle and assault, they had neither persistence nor discipline, were negligent and unreliable as sentries, and all but useless for lengthy and difficult undertakings. The financial organization of the army was as follows: The colonel and the captain bought their commissions, and sold the other commissions for as much as they could get; for equipment and for the maintenance of the troops they received a given sum of money, or, as a rule, drafts on the treasuries of particular Estates or Communes. Almost all the officers tried to make or save money by such means; and since they were always short of money, and the pay or the drafts arrived unpunctually or not at all, the soldiers plundered and robbed, while the officers extorted what they could; and enormous numbers deserted, especially after a defeat. There were hardly such things as *étapes*; the commissariat and the ambulance services were bad, and the organization of reinforcements was insufficient. Under Richelieu, who took endless trouble over the matter, there was the beginning of an army organization, which was first really developed and completed by the ministers for war, Tellier and Louvois, under Mazarin and Louis XIV. Drill and training were insufficient to produce thoroughly disciplined troops. There was also a lack of leaders; the generals whom Richelieu placed in command—the Maréchals de Chatillon, La Force, and Brézé, the Prince de Condé and Cardinal la Valette—failed to distinguish themselves, and accomplished little or nothing.

At this period the Dutch and Swedish armies, thanks to the creative genius of the two princes of Orange, and of Gustavus Adolphus, were far superior to all others in military value, training, discipline, and advanced tactics. The French army, which by the close of the seventeenth century was to become the pattern for all other armies, could not, in those days, be compared with the Dutch and Swedish troops; the Imperial army was far better. The only French commander who accomplished anything in these years was the Duke of Weimar, who, in October 1635, entered the French service with his eighteen thousand German soldiers, in consideration of a yearly payment of four million livres, and the promise that on the conclusion of peace he should be Landgrav of Alsace; and besides him, the former leader of the Huguenots, the Duc de Rohan, who was now commanding the French troops in the Grisons, must also be mentioned.

Campaigns consisted essentially of a wearisome warfare of sieges and mutual exhaustion, and were almost always interrupted in winter. The first year's fighting brought the minister disappointment after disappointment. The anticipated conspiracy in Belgium did not lead to an outbreak; its few leaders were captured; and the northern army melted almost completely away in the autumn. In the following year the Imperial troops captured the fortress of Corbie and advanced as far as Compiègne. There was great alarm in Paris, and angry rebellion against the ministers; scornful placards were printed, abusing the Cardinal, and he was hissed as he drove by. The king's expression was gloomy. Richelieu, already unwell, was disheartened; he had had serious trouble of different kinds with his own family, and was receiving bad news from the other battle-fields also. He began to have doubts about his work and his success; he had a slight nervous breakdown, but quickly recovered, and set to work again with the utmost energy. At this time the exhortations of Père Joseph are said to have given him comfort; he drove through the city and encouraged the people by his calm. Volunteers were enrolled on every side, and horses commandeered; the king took the field with 40,000 foot and 14,000 horse, to which were added the 8,000 men of the household troops, and Picardy was cleared again. It is recorded that from this time forward Richelieu displayed a profounder piety in his life and thoughts and all his activities.

On September 18, 1636, after prolonged hostilities on either side, the Emperor declared war on France. Three months later he died, and his son Ferdinand III was elected Roman Emperor on February 15, 1637. All attempts to influence the Electors of Saxony, Brandenburg, and Bavaria against this election were fruitless.

The longing for peace was growing amidst the oppressed populations. The troops of the Thirty Years' War, where the peasants and farmers were concerned, were organized and irresistible robber-bands. The passage of an army, a regiment, a squadron, whether of enemy troops or friendly, meant burning, looting, and ill-usage; the crops, far and near, ripe or unripe, were cut as forage for the horses, the best of food was demanded for the men, money was extorted, and everything that could be of any service was carried off. Endless atrocities, too, were committed, and there was much wilful destruction. These were the soldiers whom Grimmelshausen called "human wolves." "On my estate all the peasants have been beaten until they are cripples," writes a nobleman in the neighbourhood of Paris after such troops have gone by. "Every girl, every woman in the village is lost," we read in another report. Year after year such troops passed through the frontier provinces.

Negotiations were carried on incessantly; secret agents of the Emperor and of the French and Spanish Governments went in disguise to the hostile Courts, with special passports, lived in concealment under false names, and were received in secret; but no agreement was ever reached.

The war aims of Oxenstjerna were Pomerania and the overlordship of the Baltic; Holland demanded the recognition of her independence; Richelieu's aims were the permanent possession of Pinerolo and the Valtellina, the three bishoprics, and Lorraine, and the safeguarding of the "German liberties," which meant the impotence of the Emperor within the Empire. All negotiations with Spain were wrecked on the first two demands, and on the Spanish minister's jealousy of Richelieu, and his hopes of Louis XIII, and of Richelieu's death. Over and over again Richelieu proposed an armistice of ten or twelve years, but on the basis of the *status quo*, so that the territories of which he was in occupation might be retained for that length of time. The other parties would not agree.

RICHELIEU'S WAR POLICY

In October 1636 the Holy See sent Cardinal Ginetti to Cologne, in order to convoke a peace congress; but since the German princes who were fighting on the side of France and Sweden were regarded as rebels, their representatives were refused such passes as should have been issued to equally privileged and belligerent Powers, and the congress never assembled.

The Duke of Mantua died; Parma concluded peace with Spain; Duke Victor Amadeus died in Savoy. Both his brothers, Prince Thomas and Cardinal Maurice, had Spanish sympathies, and his widow, Christine, the sister of Louis XIII, being advised by the Jesuit father Monot, who had long disliked Richelieu on personal grounds, would not hear of French help and protection. In his reports to the king Richelieu expressed himself in the most wrathful and uncourtier-like terms over the "extravagances, blindness, and self-will" of the Duchess; and Savoy too became a battle-field.

For a year nothing was achieved. There was some idea of marrying the Princess Maria Gonzaga to the Polish king, in order to secure Poland as an ally; there were thoughts of the Turks, and negotiations with Ráckóczy. The treaties with Sweden were constantly renewed; and continually Richelieu drew fresh forces from his country. In 1637 France arrayed six armies, with a total strength of 122,000 men. Nevertheless, in the north the incapable La Valette had no success, and a simultaneous thrust of Banér and Bernhard of Weimar against Austria failed, because the reinforcements from France did not arrive in time.

RICHELIEU

At last, on March 2, 1638, Bernhard was victorious at Rhinefeld, where Johann von Werth, Savelli, and two other Bavarian and Imperial generals were captured by the French; and on December 17th of the same year he took Breisach. This was a great success, because the fortress not only barred the way from bank to bank of the Rhine, but, above all, cut the connection between the Spanish Netherlands and Italy, so that the possession of the Swiss passes could no longer be of advantage to the Spaniards. But Bernhard, who regarded himself not as a general in the French service, but as an ally of France, was unwilling to hand over the fortress to France without more ado. This caused Richelieu great anxiety, and when the duke offered to conquer Lorraine and the Franche Comté for him, he dared not agree to his proposal. But Bernhard of Weimar died only six months later, on July 18, 1639. Richelieu lost his best general, but was rid of a heavy anxiety, all the more so because the duke's troops entered the French service under the Swiss General von Erlach, and with them Breisach likewise came to France.

So gradually the change came about, as a result of fortunate occurrences for which France could not have waited but for Richelieu's unexampled perseverance and his labours; and as a result of the war itself, which was turning the French troops into real soldiers. In 1640 Casale was occupied and Turin taken; the adroitness of Mazarini, who a year earlier had entered the French service, brought about a reconciliation with the Duchess of Savoy, and drew Prince Thomas over to the French side. The French fleet, which Richelieu had created, and which now numbered over a hundred sail, cut out a Spanish gold transport in the same year, and defeated the Spanish fleet off Cadiz. What was even more important was that in Spain, weakened and exhausted by endless wars, Catalonia and Portugal were in revolt, and French troops invaded Spain itself. It was the long war, and the experience obtained thereby, that at last placed able commanders at the head of the French army, such as the Maréchal de Guébriant, and the even more notable Turenne, and the Duc d'Enghien, who reached eminence only after Richelieu's death.

With these successes the French war aims grew more ambitious; the war, which had really been commenced as a war of defence against the threatening power of the house of Habsburg, now assumed the form of a war of conquest. Richelieu got his jurists and archivists to prepare documentary proof of France's right to Milan, Naples, Sicily, Burgundy, and Piedmont; not that he wished to conquer them all, for he was extremely cautious and moderate in his policy of annexation; but he thought that one should demand a great deal more than one obtained. He had serious thoughts of the county of Roussillon on the Spanish frontier, and of the Flemish provinces, and no longer considered it impossible to retain Alsace, which was in the first place to have been a security merely. And he now allowed it to be represented that warfare is a legitimate mode of acquisition. Thus he prepared the way for the peace negotiations.

On December 28, 1641, the preliminary peace was concluded at Hamburg, and three months later the actual peace negotiations between the ambassadors of all the belligerent Powers, including, on this occasion, even the Protestant Estates, were to commence in Osnabrück and Münster.

But now Richelieu was no longer striving for peace. Rather he was increasing his armaments to the utmost. He wished, first of all, to attain more decisive successes. He achieved these successes, and still no peace was concluded.

CHAPTER XII

THE ADMINISTRATION

When Richelieu thus set his hand to the destinies of Europe and transformed the international status of France, he did so in the midst of incessant obstacles and difficulties of a domestic nature. He squeezed out endless sums of money for the war; he drew a mighty fleet and army from the reluctant country, forced it to monstrous efforts, and enormously increased its power; he wounded and misgoverned France in order to force her to the goal which he perceived, and France repaid him with fame and hatred.

Richelieu's position cannot in any way be compared with that of a prime minister, and hardly with that of an imperial chancellor, to such an extent were all the other ministers merely subordinates and executive instruments; he concerned himself with every branch of the administration, and did all that he could himself, in the conviction of the man of genius that the others would not do what he wanted well enough, and in his restless anxiety about his work for France. He was Foreign Minister, Home Secretary, Minister for War, Minister of the Marine, Minister of Trade and Commerce, Minister of Public Worship and Instruction, all in one person; although in matters of detail many a burden was taken off his shoulders. The administration, the war department, the generals and their enterprises, all negotiations with foreign

Powers, the proceedings at the European Courts, ecclesiastical affairs, serious lawsuits or prosecutions, and personal questions of every kind—from the world-shaking events at the seat of war to the pettiest intrigues and scandals at Court—everything came before him, was reported to him, was by him decided. Of the four secretaries of State, the one-eyed and unamiable Abel Servien, formerly intendant in Bordeaux, was secretary for war from 1630 to 1636, but the decision rested always with Richelieu himself. During that time, justly or unjustly, he was held responsible for the failures of the army; the intendant of finances, Bullion, and he mutually accused one another; there were parties in the Cabinet, and since the two Bouthilliers and Père Joseph were opposed to Servien, he fell, and an engineer officer, Sublet de Noyers, replaced him—a very honest man, without personality; an anxious place-hunter, but very good in his profession. Léon Bouthillier and his son Chavigny served the Cardinal principally in foreign affairs, though there Père Joseph was his most important collaborator and adviser. The other two secretaries of State, Brienne and La Vrillière, did not possess his confidence in the same degree, and were not given tasks of essential importance. The departments of finance and justice were more independent, though completely subordinate to him. The Seal, after Châteauneuf's imprisonment, was entrusted to Pierre Séguier, who bore a remarkable outward resemblance to his predecessor, but was very different from that self-conscious person. As a minister he was always a perfectly obedient tool, who crawled to those above him and was harsh and arrogant to

THE ADMINISTRATION

those beneath him; as a judge he was bloodthirsty and merciless.

The finances were administered by the Maréchal de Schomberg, and then by d'Effiat; when the latter died, in 1632, he was followed by Claude de Bullion, a small, stout, unappetizing man, who came of a family of officials. A man of a certain broad, not over-nice, easy-going humour, he bore with every whim and insult of the often overworked and irritable ministers, and was indispensable to them. Bullion was close and pertinacious, and knew how to make money. "In matters of finance I am aware of my complete ignorance," wrote the Cardinal of himself; in this department, therefore, he was guided entirely by his people.

In the first year of his ministry he had drafted plans of administrative reform—plans not of an alteration of the system, but of improvements; but in the stress of events they were pigeon-holed, or were carried out only in so far as his inclinations and his choice of instruments took effect in the same direction.

The great nobles, who were accustomed to being consulted, were consulted no longer; they did not submit without opposition; during the whole of his period of government there was a hard-fought and sanguinary contest; but the indomitable priest was victorious, and their opposition was annihilated; and by this victory he brought the Middle Ages to a close. Men of humble origin were appointed ministers. For all other positions he preferred the nobles, but he required absolute obedience. He did not train men, he unmade them; he began what Louis XIV completed; the two of them broke the back of the French nobility, who until then had been not courtiers, but blithe, insubordinate lords and warriors.

He had planned a reformation of the ecclesiastical administration, and even in this direction a good deal was accomplished, although time was lacking for a systematic alteration by the nomination of ecclesiastics, which was his method of procedure. Richelieu was a good Catholic—unlike Mazarin, to whom religion was a matter of the utmost indifference. With his keen, calm intellect he was able to combine an unshaken faith; perhaps because doubt was alien and unacceptable to the whole character of the man; because he simply would not admit of a critical examination of the bases of an authority hallowed by tradition. He was capable of great inward resignation and exaltation, which for him was a source of energy and will. He believed in relics and in vows, and he pledged himself in writing to have a Mass said every Sunday in the Château de Richelieu if God and the Apostle John would rid him within a week of his terrible headaches. He placed France under the protection of the Holy Virgin. Nevertheless, his plans of ecclesiastical reform did not aim at the ideal which so many were seeking to attain, of confining the clergy to matters spiritual. He had employed ecclesiastics as councillors, ambassadors, ministers, generals, and admirals. None of his collaborators had such political influence as the Capucin, Père Joseph, whom he appointed minister, but for whom he was unable to obtain a cardinalate from Rome. Père Joseph was likewise his adviser in all ecclesiastical affairs.

Richelieu was thoroughly conscious of his quality as a Cardinal of the Church of Rome, although he never went to Rome, and in political matters was by no means submissive to Rome. As a Cardinal he insisted on his precedence over even the princes of the Royal house. He prevented Gallicanism from tampering with the religious principles of the Church, but as minister he upheld the privileges of the Gallican Church, which were really the privileges of the French kings. He would not have the dogmas and doctrines of the Church infringed; he desired its unity, and wrote in favour of the union of the Churches, which to him, as an absolutist, centralizing minister, must have seemed a desirable goal; even though he was wise enough to regard any compulsion, in matters of conscience, of so numerous and powerful a sect as the Protestant, as useless and mischievous. Richelieu would never have committed the follies of Louis XIV. He would not permit Ultramontanism or the Church to exert any disturbing influence on French policy; but under the influence of Père Joseph he suppressed those religious movements which the Church regarded as dangerous. The lax and enthusiastic Illuminati were suppressed equally with the austere Jansenists. As a young man he had known the first leader of the Jansenists in France, the fiery Abbé of Saint-Cyran, Duvergier de Hauranne; the two men had been on very good terms, and Richelieu had thought of giving the other a bishopric; but when the Abbé told Vincent de Paul that there had been no Church for the last six centuries, and others that St. Thomas and the scholastics had destroyed the true knowledge of God, and that Luther had erred only in form and not in principle when he denied the invalidity of the marriage of the Duc d'Orléans, and when in connection with certain political questions the king displayed scruples which could be traced to the influence of St-Cyran, Richelieu had him arrested (on May 14, 1638) and taken to the prison of Vincennes. "I have to-day done that about which people will make a great noise," said the Cardinal to his chief gentleman-usher, the Abbé Beaumont de Pèrefixe; "I have had the Abbé de St-Cyran arrested. But I am conscious of having performed a service to State and Church. If Luther and Calvin had been locked up when they first began to announce new doctrines, how much mischief and disorder would the world have been spared!"

In the selection of bishops he saw to it that they were not only pious men but fit for administrative duties, and the bishops appointed by him were mostly nobles. It was the common and pernicious custom of the bishops to live in Paris instead of in their dioceses; this custom he vigorously opposed; but he was ready to pardon worldly behaviour in those who were subservient to him in politics, and who, on the granting of State subsidies in the assemblies of the clergy, voted for large sums. He took pains to ensure the suitability of priests, and promoted the better education of clerics by founding seminaries. He reduced the number of convents, and when necessary he introduced reforms, for monastic discipline had been everywhere greatly relaxed; he had himself elected

> Monfrere, Je suy outré de la mort
> de Monsr le Mareschal D'effiat
> pour la perte qui ont faite le
> Roy, la france, moy et mes Amys
> particuliers. Je supplie Dieu qu'il
> me console en cette affliction qui
> est une des plus grandes qui eust
> peu m'arriver, Et me donne lieu
> de vous tesmoigner que Je suy
> Monfrere
>
> Vostre tresaffectionné frere
> a vous rendre service
> Le Card. de Richelieu

FACSIMILE OF A LETTER OF RICHELIEU'S TO THE MARÉCHAL DE MAILLÉ-BRÉZÉ
(*Nationalbibliothek, Vienna*)

coadjutor of the Order of Cluny, and he wanted to become the General of all the Benedictine Orders in France—for the sake of power as much as for that of reform—but this the Pope would not allow. In every province he accomplished much, though he was nowhere able completely to overcome the opposition to his measures; and always and everywhere he proceeded, consciously or unconsciously, in the first place as a statesman, and only in the second place as a priest; the political interests took precedence of all others.

To that upper stratum of the Third Estate which consisted of the nobility of the robe he was not well disposed; the rest of the nation was powerless and merely an object of government. Under the reforms which he had planned the sale and inheritance of offices would have been abolished; but for these reforms the State needed quieter times and greater wealth than it had ever enjoyed. On the contrary, the number of saleable offices was repeatedly increased, for the sake of the profit derived from their sale; and the incumbents of the offices already existing, who were unwilling to share their power and their earnings, vigorously opposed such increase. On other grounds also there were perpetual conflicts with the Parlement; the special tribunals which were set up to condemn Richelieu's political opponents were infringements of the rights of the Parlement; moreover, the minister would not tolerate any intervention in affairs of State. Over and over again the presidents and councillors were summoned to the Louvre, where the king severely reproved them; and presidents and councillors were frequently banished, or removed from their posts, or arrested. In the edict of February 21, 1641, which the Parlement was forced to register, it was "forbidden for all future time to concern itself with affairs of State." The leadership of the State, the policy of the country in the real sense of the word, was reserved to "the king himself, and the queen, and his successors"; in financial matters and other governmental affairs the Parlement retained the right to make representations, but if the king rejected these his will had to be done.

The existing state of affairs was, as a matter of fact, untenable. The incomplete constitution of the Middle Ages, in which complicated rights and privileges infringed one another, and embarrassing vestiges of ancient institutions, together with the undeveloped commencements of new institutions, filled the administrative arena with overgrown fragments, was in all respects inadequate. The indefinite situation of the Parlement, its intricate and contradictory functions as court of justice, administrative authority, and State chancellery, made it too weak to exercise control, but strong enough to cause disturbance. In the provinces the autonomous magistracies and municipalities were an obstacle to a unitarian administration. Not systematically, but whenever they proved a hindrance, or refused to grant the necessary funds, or refused to dissolve, Richelieu suppressed their privileges. Here again Louis XIV completed what Richelieu began. The old *Magistrature*, together with the Estates, or in their stead, had long and repeatedly defended the "unwritten Constitution" of France against the monarchy. But it was an obstacle to the unity of the realm, to an ordered administration, to any strong and purposeful Government. The worst of it was that instead of reforming institutions that were in its way, this Government overturned and destroyed them.

In order to watch over and enforce the execution of its decrees, the Government sent into the provinces—and also to the armies—its intendants, commissaries with extraordinary and often unlimited powers, against which the old authorities and the Parlements waged a bitter warfare, although the intendants were mostly taken from their ranks. Richelieu had not created them, but he made extensive use of them. They were the organs of his policy, which watched over all things and prevailed in all. Under Louis XIV the intendants became permanent officials; the old authorities were more and more weakened and thrust aside by them, and the modern, centralized administration has been evolved from them.

By the complete downfall of the Estates, legislation was entirely transferred to the monarchy. And it shows us how far the vitality of the medieval institutions, was destroyed, and therewith the germ of the modern constitution, that the only codification of Richelieu's time, the collection of statutes published by Michel de Marillac in his capacity of keeper of the Seal, which the jurists of the Parlement scornfully nicknamed the *Code Michaud*, complied almost completely with the demands of the Estates of 1614 and the Notables of 1627, and was given the force of law.

Richelieu's aims were always grandiose and authoritative. France was to become rich and powerful. He endeavoured to promote commerce and industry, to limit the imports of goods from abroad, and to increase exports. He founded great companies which received the monopoly of overseas trade with all parts of the world. But the companies failed, and, as regards the colonies, only the religious missions had any real significance. Capital was insufficient; private initiative small; unlike the Englishman and the Dutchman, the sedentary Frenchman, accustomed to the sweets of home, seldom felt the desire to go trading in remote and perilous countries; and since Governmental decrees could not replace economic initiative, could not create organizations or achieve results, Richelieu was powerless to increase the sources of wealth; only the power which was his gift to France indirectly augmented the wealth of the country. But it was long before this was perceptible. At first he created fresh and increased poverty. In the beginning he had expressed the desire to lighten the burden of taxation; his wars increased it intolerably. The method of levying taxation was inept and senseless. Economic science was only groping towards the light; men had not yet learned by experience. The revenues of the State were based on old and long superannuated laws and institutions, or on expedients inspired by necessity; a confused and disorderly hodge-podge, which had largely lost all meaning; law had everywhere become injustice; the heaviest taxes were imposed on poverty. The method of levying was the most costly conceivable, and the collection was disgraced by every kind of arbitrariness, every imaginable abuse; it swallowed up an immoderate portion of the yield, and another portion was consumed by the contractors; little was left over for the State. The internal customs on the provincial frontiers and at the city gates imposed a serious and senseless burden and impediment on trade and commerce. The indirect taxes, everywhere different, were imposed in some places and not in others; the tax on salt, the famous *gabelle*, was imposed in a number of provinces and not in others. The farmers of taxes became millionaires, and to make them so thousands of poor people who could not pay their taxes died in prison. Armies of customs officers fought armies of smugglers; a third of all the criminals in the galleys were sentenced for smuggling salt.

In this connection Richelieu's rule brought no improvement, no alleviation. The deficit, which in 1624 amounted to ten million livres, had by 1639 increased to fifty-six millions. Loans were raised at usurious interest, which sometimes was not paid or was enormously reduced, and no attempt was made to cope with this state of affairs other than by fresh taxation. The consequences were even more serious revolts on the part of the oppressed population. In 1631 the vine-dressers rose in Burgundy; in 1632 a regiment had to be sent to Lyons, and several persons were hanged there; in 1635 there was a peasant rising in the south-west; in 1636 followed the insurrection of the *Croquants* in the middle provinces, against whom a small army had to be sent under the Duc de La Valette; and a battle was fought in which 1,200 rebellious peasants and workmen fell at the barricades. Even more violent was the revolt of the *Va-nu-pieds*, when in 1638 the salt-tax was about to be introduced in the already heavily burdened Normandy. At the head of the people was an ex-priest, who gave himself the name of Jean Va-nu-pieds, John Barefoot. First they murdered the tax-farmers and collectors; finally they plundered the shops and houses of Rouen; the bourgeois armed themselves, killed many of the insurgents, and suppressed the revolt. Since the whole population was at heart on the side of the Va-nu-pieds, the Courts did not proceed against them with great severity. The movement was practically extinct when in November Colonel Gassion marched into the province with four thousand men, and a criminal assize was held. The chancellor Seguiér appeared in Rouen, and proceeded with all the cruelty which was the obverse of his creeping humility towards the mighty. The Parlement was suspended; the prisoners were executed without inquiry. Richelieu himself, who with the years grew ever harsher and more despotic, and more embittered by any opposition, came at length to conceive the notion that oppression and misery were quite in order; that the people, if things went well with them, would be utterly disobedient and could not be induced to fulfil their obligations.

CHAPTER XIII

THE DEPOPULATED COURT

ALL public activities met with endless opposition. For the reigning minister there were two fields of activity: one, the country which he ruled and administered, was the object and the instrument of his schemes; the other was the narrower field of the Court, from which he had to direct his operations, and in which he must remain; and which, because in those days it was the sole source of power, might become more dangerous to him than the millions who unwillingly obeyed him.

His relations with the king were unchanged; they were never perfectly secure. And the king was still the one who decided; Richelieu might make the most colossal plans, might achieve tremendous things, but however great the impression produced on the king, however greatly he might influence him, a whim of the monarch's might defeat him. He had never dreamed of rebelling against the king, so that every caprice was of significance for him. In the autumn of 1635 the king wanted to join the army; Richelieu was too ill to follow him, and wished therefore to hold him back; the king lost his temper, and Richelieu gave way. Thereupon Bouthillier wrote to him: "The king believes that you are angered. For God's sake, if you have written anything that may give him this belief, allow us to hold back the letter!" Meanwhile a letter from the king had arrived: *"Mon Cousin,"* he wrote—for as cardinal and peer of France Richelieu had a right to this form of address—"I am in despair over the heedlessness with which I wrote to you yesterday concerning my journey. I beg of you, burn the letter and forget what it contained. Believe that I did not intend to anger you, and that I am willing unconditionally and precisely to follow your good advice." The two men feared one another, and neither could endure that the other should complain; each was somehow in the other's power. In public they treated each other with conspicuous gestures of the greatest courtesy. When in 1633 the Cardinal was made a knight of the Holy Ghost, the king, after the banquet given for the new knights, had a perfect mountain of sweetmeats presented to the Cardinal, out of which sprang a perfumed fountain. The Cardinal had an equestrian statue of the king erected in the Place Royale, then the most fashionable promenade of Paris; "in token of gratitude," one might read on the pedestal, "for so good a ruler and so magnanimous a monarch, who has overwhelmed him with honours and benefits"; but under this inscription, always eager for his own praise, he had engraved a sonnet by his own Court poet, Desmarets, in which Louis XIII says:

> Armand, the great Armand, the soul of my government,
> Bore my arms and my commandments afar;
> From him the fame in whose radiance I walk. . . .

For in the intimate, everyday life of the Court, the Cardinal caused the king "much trouble." Louis XIII, on the other hand, often took pleasure in annoying his minister with trivialities. He could not endure some of the Cardinal's confidants, and found their manners bad; if the Cardinal over and over again compelled the king to dismiss people whom he trusted and wished to benefit, so on occasion the king was able to harass the Cardinal, but was unable to get his way; Richelieu did not dismiss capable and devoted servants. Servien, whose loud and unpleasing manner of speech annoyed the king, was not dismissed on that account, but only when Père Joseph and the two Bouthilliers united against him and brought about his downfall.

The king conceived timid and irresolute fancies for certain of the queen's ladies. The first of these was Mlle. de Hauteforte, a proud, handsome blonde, who laughed at her shy, kingly admirer; but Richelieu, who knew that she could not endure him, spent many an anxious hour before he could make an end of the affair. A few years later it was Mlle. de Lafayette, a gentle, dark-haired girl, who returned the king's love in her quiet fashion, and to whom the troubled monarch unburdened his heart. When Richelieu had it suggested to her that she should influence the king in accordance with his instructions, and she indignantly refused, an ugly intrigue drove the girl into a convent. The Dominican father, Carré, one of Richelieu's most dangerous tools, was instructed to inspire her with fears for the welfare of her soul. From this time onwards the melancholy king often went to the convent of the Daughters of the Visitation of the Virgin Mary and, sitting by the grille, conversed with the girl, who had now become Sœur Angélique.

The Catholic party at Court likewise gave the Cardinal much trouble, chiefly, however, on isolated occasions. Père Caussin, who since 1636 had been the king's confessor, endeavoured to excite his abhorrence of the minister's policy, the cruelty of the long war, and the alliance with the Protestants, and exhorted him to seek reconciliation with his mother. With the most honourable intentions, the pious father opposed the cardinal-politician; after fervent prayer, and in tears, he declared that he had told the king only what he owed it to his conscience to tell him. He was dismissed and banished to Rennes, and the Jesuits came near to losing their privilege of furnishing one of their Order to be the king's confessor.

Of the royal house one member only, the Prince de Condé, was subservient to the Cardinal. He had the nature of a trickster, and with the insight of vulgar avarice he had recognized that nothing could be achieved by those who opposed this man, but that everything could be obtained through him, and he remained obedient, and even crawled before the minister. Condé, in the State as in the field, was an instrument of no great value, but he was cunning and not uneloquent, and he was the first prince of the blood. With the others there was nothing to be done. The Comte de Soissons remained obdurate and haughty, obeying only under protest, and finally left the country; he combined with the Duc de Guise and Bouillon, the son of the man who had given so much trouble to Richelieu, and to others before him, and invaded France with his own and some Spanish troops. On July 6, 1641, there was a battle near

Sedan, in which the prince was killed by a pistol-bullet.

The Duc d'Orléans, directly he heard of Montmorency's execution, had once more left the country. In Nancy he fell in love with the sister of Duke Charles, Margaret of Lorraine, and on January 3, 1632, he secretly married her. When he made his peace with the Court nothing was known of his marriage; but the rumour gradually reached Paris. The Duc de Puylaurens, his first gentleman-in-waiting, who for the moment was Gaston's favourite, and had advised him to contract the marriage, became alarmed, and alarmed the duke himself and urged him to fly; he went to Brussels, to the queen-mother, where both were well received by the Infanta Clara Isabella Eugenia. The Infanta allowed him a pension of 30,000 guilders, and when his young wife, disguised as a man, with a pass belonging to her brother, the Duke Nicholas Francis, made her way through the French lines and joined him in Brussels, the Infanta increased the pension to 45,000 guilders. Richelieu and the king were furious; Charles of Lorraine was an enemy, and the heir to the throne had not the right to marry without the king's consent; the Paris Parlement declared that since on this ground the contract was null, the marriage was invalid; but, since the wedding had been duly performed in church, the Pope recognized it as valid. The couple remained for two years in Brussels; then the Infanta died; dissensions arose between mother and son, and still more between their respective followers, and these led to actual fighting and attempted murder; all suffered from ennui, and felt that they were disliked in Belgium; and so Gaston secretly returned to France, and begged for pardon; and after the Cardinal had listened to the last detail of his doings, and he had betrayed and abandoned all his friends, and even his mother, he was once more pardoned and given money, and towards his protectors in Brussels he played the same sorry part as he had always played. "If only he had told me, so that I might with due courtesy have given him an escort!" said the Spanish governor, the Marques de Aytona, with Spanish calm.

In order to assure himself against Orléans, and to avoid future difficulties, Richelieu thought it best to buy the ambitious Puylaurens, who had absolute power over Monsieur. The Cardinal married him to his own niece, the younger Mlle. de Pontchâteau, and made him a duke and a peer of France. But he must very quickly have formed the opinion that Puylaurens was betraying him, for a few weeks after the wedding the Cardinal invited him to a Court banquet in his room, and had much conversation with him, teasing him and jesting; then he went out, and in his place returned Captain de Gordes, who informed Puylaurens that he was under arrest, and escorted him to the prison of Vincennes, which he never left again. Dark and tragic stories were told of his end. Various reports stated that on waking one morning he found the room dark; all the shutters were closed; he made a light and, reaching for a book he found, instead of the novels which he was accustomed to read, only devotional works; the commandant of the watch, Balouet, on being called,

THE DEPOPULATED COURT

informed him that this was according to orders, and admonished him to think of his spiritual welfare. Then he threw himself back on his pillows in despair. Two months later he died of "purple fever." Rumour, as always, attributed his death to a different cause.

For nine years Gaston lived apart from his wife; only after Richelieu's death could she venture to come to Court. Like his first wife, she bore him only daughters; and on each occasion Louis XIII was full of scornful triumph when he heard the news, and remembered his brother's great hopes. Warned and well watched, sometimes contented and sometimes complaining, the duke lived for his love affairs, and the dull or witty conversations and the intrigues of his dissolute little Court. The people knew him for what he was, as drinking, whistling, singing the street ditties—as Tallemant said, "an eternal youth"—smiling and shameless, he passed through life. From time to time the Cardinal reproached him for his manner of life and his blasphemous oaths; and when, without leave, he dismissed M. d'Elbène, the Cardinal's confidant at his Court, because he was sick of being watched, the minister wrote to him as follows: "Your highness will not wonder if I tell you frankly that you deserve a sound reprimand." It is clear that the minister was not loved at his Court, and was spoken of with scorn and hostility in his most intimate circle. But once, when Chavigny, who was fickle and easily led away, spoke in the same fashion and told some anecdote ridiculing his master, Monsieur smiled, and said: "*Et tu, fili?*" His daughter by his first marriage, Mlle. de Montpensier, knew by heart all the satirical songs about Richelieu, and was profoundly annoyed to think that he was her godfather.

The queen-mother remained in banishment. When she fell ill an officer was dispatched with a cold letter to "our honoured lady and mother," to make inquiry as to the state of her health; and he was told beforehand precisely what he was to say. Concerning the Cardinal, the queen was obstinately silent; but when war was declared on Spain she wrote letters to her son, in which the minister's policy was severely condemned. Later on she repeatedly sought to be reconciled with him, in order that she might return to France. Richelieu assured her in letters of his deepest devotion, but demanded as a preliminary the surrender of her companions and advisers, and above all of Père Chanteloube and of the Abbé de St. Germain, who had written the most venomous pamphlets against the Cardinal. To this she would not agree, and would not have been permitted to agree by the men concerned. She had not a happy life; since her temper became ever more unbearable, none of her sons-in-law would receive her. She went at last to Cologne, and lived there in comparative want, and died in what, for a queen, was poverty. "I am rejoiced to see from your letters," wrote Richelieu, when he received the news, "that she died sorely repenting her faults." He had her body conveyed to St. Denis; arrangements could be made at leisure respecting the vault and the burial; this was a task which he himself would be happy to undertake.

Thus the fortunes of all the members of the Bourbon royal family were wrecked on the tyrannical will of the priest and minister who was labouring to exalt their house. The Duke of Lorraine, a brilliant soldier at once witty, talented and foolish, reliable and faithless, had from the first leanings towards the Habsburgs, and, being irritated by Richelieu's demands, incited against the Cardinal by the ultramontanes in France, and seduced by Mme. de Chevreuse, he had adopted an anti-French policy, had taken part in Gaston's rebellion, and had given him his sister to wife. In consequence he lost his country, which in various campaigns was occupied and conquered by the French, and, since the inhabitants remained loyal to their duke, was grievously oppressed. He became an Imperial and then a Spanish general, was compelled to negotiate with France, and concluded treaties which he always broke, and had often broken even at the moment of signing. He pursued this senseless policy partly out of uncontrolled rage, but partly, we may be sure, in the belief that the house of Habsburg would eventually be victorious. But he lost the confidence of all parties; driven from his country, he drifted about as a military leader who sold himself to the highest bidder and was loyal to no one.

"Mme. de Chevreuse," said Richelieu, "has caused the ruin of the Duke of Lorraine." Doubtless the handsome lady contributed thereto. "As utterly fearless as she is utterly conscienceless, without a thought for anything but what she lusts after at the moment, without a sense of duty as she is without misgiving" —so Cardinal de Retz described her, and with all that, a bewitching woman, irresistible in her loveliness, who continued to play her sinister part. When in the beginning of the year 1629 she was permitted to return to France, she attached herself for a time to Richelieu, and even negotiated the first treaty with the Duke of Lorraine. But the Cardinal never fully trusted her. He saw with displeasure that she was as intimate as ever with Queen Anne, but since the duchess was not to be intimidated like other women, and was mistress of a thousand feminine tricks and wiles, it was impossible to get the better of her; until the Marquis de Châteauneuf, who had done the Cardinal such sanguinary service as judge, began with conspicuous assiduity to frequent her house and the apartments of the queen. Châteauneuf, a man of powerful build, with dark hair and beard, always bedecked with jewellery, was the eternal slave of women. He had already fallen in love with the lovely duchess, who made her fifty-year-old lover jealous by her deliberate flirtations with younger admirers, and even with Richelieu, of whom she averred that he, too, lay prostrate at her feet. She made the man Richelieu's enemy, made him at last so crazy with love and ambition that he betrayed State secrets, became involved with Orléans and Lorraine, and flattered himself that he could overturn the Cardinal, and even become first minister.

Meanwhile Richelieu, who was well served by his spies, was already collecting evidence against him; and as was his custom in such cases, he set down in lengthy memoranda every suspicious utterance and every dubious action which was reported to him, and, when it seemed that the fitting moment had arrived, he laid them before the king. On February 25, 1633,

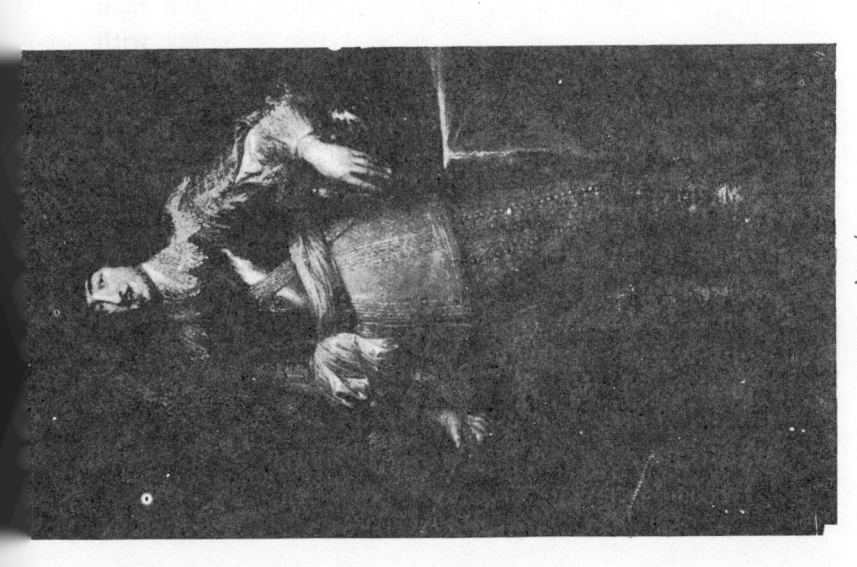

GASTON D'ORLÉANS
(Van Dyck. Musée Condé, Chantilly)

THE DUCHESSE DE CHEVREUSE
(Copper-plate engraving by Daret. Nationalbibliothek, Vienna)

the marquis was requested to give up the seals, and the captain of the guard, M. de Gordes, conveyed him to the castle of Angoulême, where he lay in prison for eleven years, until Richelieu was dead. One of his nephews and his friend the Commander de Jars were likewise arrested; others fled.

Mme. de Chevreuse was banished to Touraine. The octogenarian Archbishop Bertrand, who had once procured for Richelieu his first Court appointment, and the governor, M. de Catinat, were enchanted with the brilliant luminary which made its appearance in their province. But here, too, she had suspicious visitors; her old admirer, Mr. Montague, arrived one day, and there were others; the young men were all crazy about her, and all were exploited for political ends. The duchess was fully resolved, in agreement with the queen, to work against Richelieu's policy in all the Courts of Europe. Neither of the women had the slightest understanding of politics, and they committed high treason as stupidly and frivolously as though it had been a flirtation with an admirer whom they intended to make ridiculous.

Through the queen's groom of the chambers Pierre de La Porte, and the Superior of the Val de Grace convent, which Anne had founded, her letters were forwarded to the Court of Marie de' Medici, and to the Infanta in Brussels, and even to the prime minister or *valido* of the King of Spain, the Count-Duke Olivarez. For a long time the king and the Cardinal had strong suspicions to this effect, but no proof, until on the night of August 10, 1637, La Porte was arrested near the Louvre, and a letter from the queen to the Marques de Mirabel was found on him. Accompanied by the Archbishop of Paris, Richelieu proceeded to the convent of the Val de Grace. The Mother Superior, who took to her bed and denied everything, was immediately degraded. The queen noticed, with alarm, that no one at Court greeted her or paid her any attention. She swore on the Sacrament that she had never sent letters abroad. "Come, Madame!" said Richelieu gravely. She admitted to a few trifling matters. "There is more, Madame!" said the Cardinal. Weeping and in despair, she confessed, and begged for forgiveness; the Cardinal replied that he would try to persuade the king to pardon her. Still weeping, she cried, "How good you are, my lord Cardinal!" and grasped his hand; he withdrew it in embarrassment and left the room. She had to make her full confession in writing, and solemnly promise never again to have dealings with Mme. de Chevreuse. Then the king forgave her and kissed her, and to this reconciliation it would seem that the birth of the Dauphin, Louis XIV, was due.

In the meanwhile, Mme. de Chevreuse, at Tours, received a prayer-book, bound in red, which was sent by the queen. This was the concerted signal of extreme danger. Dressed as a man, with her face stained brown, wearing false hair, with a black bandage over her forehead, she rode off, accompanied by two servants, without baggage or linen, carrying only a few rouleaux of gold in her clothing. She rode day and night, hardly halting for sleep, and on the third day, at a château belonging to the Prince de

Marsillac, later the Duc de la Rochefoucauld, the author of the *Maxims*, she was given a carriage, drove in it for two days, and then rode again and sought out people who helped her, and in Cahuzac found an old lawyer to whom Marsillac had recommended her, and who accompanied her. Everybody was struck by the handsome young cavalier who said that he was forced to fly on account of a duel; but when, on the fifth day, she dismounted from her horse, the saddle was covered with blood, and her companion began to suspect the truth. On the eleventh day she reached the Spanish frontier; she then told him who she was, and as the honest man stood before her, touched and excited, she fell on his neck and kissed him, and rode over the frontier.

She went to Madrid, where Philip IV himself is said to have fallen in love with her, and later to London. In France the Court was greatly angered by her flight; knowing her to be dangerous, it did not like her to be out of the country. She was offered her pardon, and was requested to return; but she was distrustful, wrote mendacious and ironical letters, held Richelieu up to ridicule, paid her debts, and did not return. Her despairing husband, always in dread of being compromised by her, paid court to the Cardinal in every possible way, sent him venison and other presents, but dispatched no money to his wife—he himself had nothing but debts—and at length, in May, after receiving a handsome advance for the expenses of the journey, he went to London to fetch her; but by then she had fled to Flanders. In Dunkirk, where she found herself stranded without means, she began to see her position in another light, and wrote to Paris, to the king, the queen, and Richelieu, begging for permission to return; but she had gone too far; they were too greatly angered; and her letters were no longer answered. Then she went to Brussels, threw herself into all the intrigues that were afoot, and took part in the last rebellion in France and the conspiracy against the Cardinal. Always alluring, admired, officious, and dangerous, she contrived to hinder the negotiations for peace, and wrote to the Spanish ministers, bidding them stand firm and not surrender, for Louis was ill and Richelieu dying; it was only a question of waiting a little while, for the French opposition could not continue. Richelieu himself wrote to the king on February 15, 1640, that there was nothing to be done and that no tolerable peace could be hoped for; the Chevreuse had given the Spaniards such a description of the situation in France that they would not come to terms.

No one ever caused Richelieu such vexation and trouble as this woman. In his own and in all the foreign Courts he encountered her pernicious influence. She spoiled the king's marriage, led Gaston and the Duke of Lorraine astray, drove Châteauneuf and Chalais to treason, and spread ruin everywhere. After the Cardinal's death there were many who escaped punishment; many who had been banished were able to return to France. But her return was for ever forbidden by the king, in his last will and testament, as he lay on his death-bed. "That woman is the devil!" he said, pointing with his fleshless finger to the place where her name was written.

THE DEPOPULATED COURT

In Richelieu's last years the Court was depopulated. The Duc de Montmorency, the Maréchal de Marillac, the Comte de Chalais, and many other and lesser men had ended on the block; the Maréchals de Bassompierre and Vitry, the Commander de Jars, who was reprieved on the scaffold, the Comte de Cramail, who had once been one of the "seventeen seigneurs" who set the fashion, and who had spoken against the Cardinal, now languished in the Bastille, and Châteauneuf lay in the castle of Angoulême; the whole house of Guise and the house of Vendôme were banished, and so were the Duc d'Épernon, the Duc de Chevreuse, the Maréchal d'Estrées, and the Prince de Marsillac; the Duc de La Valette was a fugitive in England; and in the last few years there were still further sacrifices. The king, lonely and listless, lived a doleful life; he fled society, and was reluctant to show himself in Paris. Once, in his twenty-first year, in his irrepressible joy in the roaring acclamations of *"Vive le roi!"* which, whenever he showed himself, had resounded so jubilantly on every hand, he had waved his hat in return, and answered, like a delighted child: *"Vive mon peuple!"* Now scarcely a voice was raised when he passed, and rarely was even an isolated *"Vive le roi!"* to be heard in the streets. His minister's policy had made him too greatly disliked.

CHAPTER XIV

THE HOUSE OF RICHELIEU

WHEN Richelieu became secretary of State in 1617 he built himself a modest dwelling in the Rue des Mauvaises Paroles. In 1629, a year after the taking of La Rochelle, Le Mercier began to build a palace for him in the Rue St-Honoré, which, being completed in 1636, was known as the Palais Cardinal. Before his death he presented it to the king, and after various reconstructions it became the Palais Royal; only a wing and part of a gallery of the original building are still extant. His ancestral castle of Richelieu was likewise reconstructed by Le Mercier, who transformed it into a vast château surrounded with magnificent gardens; a town was to come into being there and bear his name. The château was never quite finished, but it still stands. In the neighbourhood of Paris, in 1635, he bought from the Abbey of St-Denis the domain of Ruel, and from a citizen of Paris, one Moisset, the château which the latter possessed in Ruel. This became his favourite residence, and was famed for the park which he had laid out around it, with its grottoes and fountains, its statues and great flower-beds. This was the period of the strict French *baroque*; the châteaux which replaced the fortresses and fortified houses of an earlier period had not as yet the peaceful lightness which developed during the regency of Anne of Austria. He also had the tumble-

THE HOUSE OF RICHELIEU

down Sorbonne, whose provisor he was, pulled down, and magnificently rebuilt by Le Mercier as it stands to-day. In his châteaux he displayed his princely wealth and splendour. During the latter years of his life he enjoyed an income of more than three million livres; he drew 200,000 from his estates—he possessed two dukedoms, a principality, a marquisate, counties and baronies; two millions from his benefices—he was abbot of more than ten great abbeys; 300,000 as governor of Brittany, and as much more from other offices and from pensions. In 1630, after the fall of the queen-mother, he was created Duc de Richelieu and peer of France, and then Duc de Fronsac. In the Palais Cardinal he had his gallery of paintings. Juste d'Egmont, Poerson, Simon Vouet, and, above all, Philippe de Champaigne, worked for him. Tapestries, statues, costly furniture, and silver adorned the *salons*; the magnificence of the age found expression in the materials of the clothes he wore—satins and heavy silks, embroidered with gold, and adorned with costly lace and jewels—in the liveries of the servants, the carriages and horses, and in the pedigree dogs and hounds and the birds kept by the Cardinal-Duke—for so he was always called. Subservient nobles and priests, guards, secretaries, musicians of his household, suitors and visitors without number thronged in his ante-room and chambers.

In this environment he lived and worked. In the morning, to begin his day, he always received the director of the posts, De Nouveau, who laid before him such letters as had been intercepted and opened and seemed to contain matter of importance; the commandant of the Bastille, Du Tremblay, the brother of Père Joseph, who had to report on the prisoners of State and their conversation; and his dread chief of police, Isaac de Laffemas, with whom he discussed every suspicious movement, and all criminal proceedings, whether current or pending. With these sinister consultations the day began. Then followed the reading of the dispatches which had arrived, at which, if he was in Paris, Père Joseph was consulted. Ambassadors, envoys, and diplomatic agents were received; then he worked until eleven with Père Joseph and the secretaries of State. At eleven he entered the chapel and read Mass. For another hour he gave audience, and then came the midday meal, which was taken at a richly furnished and richly provided table. After the meal he gave further audience for a couple of hours, whereupon the private secretaries entered—Charpentier, Le Masle, Charré, or the cipher-master Rossignol; the Cardinal then wrote or dictated until the evening, read the letters that had arrived during the day, and then, until nine or ten o'clock, he conversed with his intimates: his gentleman-usher, De Beaumont, his physician, Citois, the Abbé de Boisrobert, and such others as might be present. Between nine and ten o'clock he went to bed, but usually rose again at two in the morning and worked until five.

This, if he did not happen to have audience of the king, and when banquets, ceremonies, State assemblies, and journeys did not intervene, was his day's work: terribly exhausting for this fragile Titan; and it is astounding that his frail and sickly body was able to

THE PALAIS CARDINAL
(From "*Topographia Galliæ*," Frankfort-on-Main, circa 1640)

THE MARQUIS DE CINQ-MARS
(Le Nain. *Louvre, Paris*)

endure the stupendous labours, the continual nervous strain, and the wearing excitement of his life until his fifty-eighth year. Incessant headaches, fever, a severe and painful affection of the bladder, and agonizing hæmorrhoids, and finally a general invasion of rodent ulcers, which caused him unspeakable suffering, slowly wore him down; yet all this was powerless to extinguish the electrical energy, the untamable will, the quick and resourceful intellect of the man.

This incessant strain meant exhaustion and apathy in his moments of leisure. He was afflicted by the blackest melancholy when he was not working. Sometimes, after a period of intense excitement, when he had once more won in a game played for the highest stakes, he would run roaring and neighing through the rooms, and then, bowed over the billiard-table, would remain rigid and motionless, and at last, bathed in perspiration, would throw himself down and fall asleep. His lot was no easy one, what with the strenuousness of his labours, and the opposition and the cold hatred which he encountered: when he did take a little rest he wanted to be able to laugh, and all who could cheer and amuse him were welcome—buffoons, jesters, comedians: all were welcome who could do or say anything new, and none more so than the frivolous, witty, intelligent Abbé de Boisrobert, irresistible in his careless good-nature; who knew the secret of pleasing the Cardinal, who always called him "Bois" for short; who was always falling into disgrace—once because the king complained that he had smuggled a little actress of dubious reputation into the Royal circle—but who was so sorely missed that he was always recalled by the Cardinal. Ladies of the Court were often present at these conversations; the tone of Society was freer and coarser than to-day; a witty obscenity, if not too shocking, was tolerated by ladies and priests alike.

A purely humane spirit could not prevail in this man's house; delicacy, tenderness, and cordiality were foreign to his nature. Yet he was a grateful master to those who supported him unconditionally and were completely subservient, although he could be brutal when in an evil humour, and was given to unpleasant jests; he was "the best master, kinsman, and friend," said Monglat; "if he was only sure that anyone loved him, that man's fortune was made." The man who could hate so inexorably desired to be loved; and hard as he was, the greatness of the man, and a certain grace of manner and bearing, were able to win men's hearts; the Duc de Charost, after the lapse of years, still spoke with emotion of "his kind master." But more admired than loved him, and still more execrated him. For the queen and her ladies, the princesses, and all the young people at Court he was a source of terror, the wicked man in the purple before whom they trembled.

In his testament was a curious legacy: 20,000 livres were bequeathed to the Baron de La Broye, the heir of Claude Barbin, the minister of the queen-mother, who had made him secretary of State; whom he had never allowed to return to France, and who had died in Hamburg. Did he fear the man as a possible rival? He knew him for a capable man and a man of note. Barbin had complained bitterly of his ingratitude.

The legacy would seem to be inspired by a belated qualm of conscience.

Richelieu is said to have been a lover of women. Nothing is definitely known, and it was an age of much malicious gossip; but so much was said of his love-affairs that, even though individual stories are incredible or unproven, there must have been something at the back of them. He was, after all, a human being; the ecclesiastics of his time were not strictly ascetic, and his vanity and sensitiveness were great. Nevertheless, all reports agree on one point—that he did not enjoy much success. "The man who did everything with elegance and grace was uncouth and awkward with women," says Retz. It was related of the beautiful courtesan, Marion Delorme, that she visited Ruel disguised as a page; the tale was told by many, but by no reliable witness. The greatest suspicion lay on his relations to his niece, Marie Madeleine de Vignerot, whom he afterwards created Duchesse d'Aiguillon. After the death of her husband, M. de Combalet, a captain of the Normandy regiment, who fell before Montpellier, she had wished to enter a convent, but Richelieu persuaded her to live with him. She was never remarried, and he was at all events greatly attached to her. There is something enigmatic about the historical portrait of this woman: she was noted for her great beauty, her fanatical piety, her avarice, and her revengeful nature. Whether her love for her uncle was of an unlawful character seems very doubtful; her beauty made suspicion inevitable.

Since his brother Henri, whom he loved above all

men, and the child of this brother were dead, and since his other brother, Alphonse, was a monk, he bequeathed his name to the offspring of his sister, Françoise, who had married Réné de Vignerot, Baron de Pontcourlay. The lovely Marie Madeleine was her daughter. Her son, François de Pont-Courlay, became general of the galleys. Richelieu's brother, Alphonse, although a Carthusian, was made Archbishop of Lyons and Cardinal; he was a peculiar person, slightly crazy, and sometimes believed himself to be God the Father. Of the earlier generations of the family nothing is known, but Richelieu's sister, Nicole, who married the Marquis de Maillé-Brézé, died insane. Her husband became a marshal of France. The majority of the members of the "Holy Family," as they were called in hate and derision, did not amount to much; to the Maréchal de Brézé and the young Pontcourlay Richelieu wrote in the most acrimonious tone. Pontcourlay was discharged after a few years; Brézé fell into disgrace. His son, however, the young Duc de Fronsac, was in later years to become a brilliant and victorious admiral. Richelieu's capable uncle on his mother's side, the Commander of the Maltese Order, Amador de La Porte, was appointed to important offices; his cousin, Charles de La Porte, a violent and choleric man, became grand master of artillery, and eventually Duc de La Meilleraye and marshal of France. Of his more distant relatives (on the father's side) of the house of Cambout-Pontchâteau, the Marquis de Coislin was colonel-general of the Swiss when he fell in 1641; his elder sister became the wife of the Duc de la Valette, whom Richelieu, on account of an actual or alleged failure of duty in Catalonia, had sentenced to death—for he had fled—*in effigie*; his younger sister married the Duc de Puylaurens, who died in prison, and took as her second husband the Comte de Harcourt. Another niece married the Comte de Guiche, who afterwards became the Maréchal de Gramont. The daughter of Richelieu's sister, Nicole, made the greatest marriage; the dwarfish, delicate little Clemence de Maillé-Brézé became the Duchesse d'Enghien; Condé is said to have knelt to the Cardinal, begging for her hand for his son. She was an unloved and unhappy wife, a sacrifice to fame—sacrificed to become the wife of the great Condé.

This was his family. The world showed him two faces; he knew that a sea of enmity surrounded him, that he was constantly threatened by conspiracies and murderous designs. At last he went even to the king surrounded by his guards, and under silk and purple he is said to have worn a shirt of mail as a protection against the assassin's dagger. But wherever he appeared all bowed flatteringly before him, doing homage to the "great Armand," as he loved to hear himself called; he loved praise, and took pains to ensure that in the newspapers, which were then in their infancy—in the annual *Mercure François* and the weekly *Gazette de France*, which was published by Théophraste Renaudot, and to which he and the king sometimes contributed—as in his *Memoirs*, events were represented as he desired, and that his part in them was duly extolled. The king was told how happy he was to have such a minister, and in one commissioned article it was said that four centuries often passed without the birth of such a genius. But his love of literature—and chiefly the drama—was perhaps not wholly inspired by the desire for fame. His taste, it is true, was bad. This was the period when French literature was achieving form, and from its former indiscipline was evolving into the narrow academic constraint of the time of Louis XIV. Yet a freer and bolder spirit still prevailed. Balzac and Voiture—and, if we take account of the next generation, St. Evremond and Pascal—were creating French prose, in which Richelieu's polemical and theological writings do not cut at all a bad figure. Malherbe, who died in the year of the taking of La Rochelle, had purified the poetical vocabulary, and, without being a great poet, had bridled a nobler and more powerful Pegasus. Corneille was writing his first plays.

Boisrobert, who was a delightful talker, but nothing to boast of as a writer, was at the same time Richelieu's literary secretary; he was allowed to chatter away about anything, and, good-natured fellow that he was, employed this privilege to the benefit of many. A whole tribe of literary men—mostly of small account—were in Richelieu's service, or sponged on him. Boisrobert used to attend regular conferences of certain persons of no great significance, at which literary matters were discussed. Richelieu, who liked to see everything done according to rule, transformed these conferences—by no means to the unmixed joy of those who took part in them—into the French Academy, with the function, as it says in the statutes, "of making the French language the most perfect of modern tongues." St. Evremond, at that time a young cavalry officer, promptly derided it in a thoroughly witty comedy, which—after the Cardinal's death—was passed from hand to hand in the *salons* and read with great enjoyment. The Academy, at Richelieu's behest, was immediately forced to make war on the greatest living poet of the age—Corneille. It is uncertain whether the Cardinal's enmity was based on personal vanity or on political grounds—because the subject of *Le Cid* was Spanish, and because it glorified an enemy of the realm. For Richelieu himself wanted to become an author. In the Palais Cardinal, as at Ruel, he had a theatre built. He wrote sketches for plays, which were worked out for him by certain more or less talented writers, and, above all, by his own household poet, Desmarets de Sorlin, and were then performed by the company of the Théâtre Bourgogne, before the Court and invited guests, who had to admire both the play and the author. Altogether, he spent a great deal on the theatre, and did a great deal towards making it the fashion. It is astonishing that he could find the necessary time. It was a hobby, and even though his relation to such intellectual matters was not wholly genuine, and though much that was petty in his character was revealed thereby, yet this hobby of his made for the promotion of culture. This was the age when Paris was absorbing all the intellectual life of the country; and the ideal of a great France with the capital as its light-giving centre became a living reality very largely as a result of Richelieu's efforts. And although the Parisians jested in secret over the hobbies and pretensions of the "Eminentissimus," as they malevolently called him, yet in his wealth and magnificence and pomp, as in his private life and his conversation, he never gave the impression of a parvenu, as did Concini before him and Mazarin after, but was always, from the first, a very great seigneur.

So he lived, a sick man, but indomitably active; with the harsh lines deepening in the small, deadly pale face, with its little pointed beard, now rapidly growing white; his thin, decaying body swathed in purple or silk; surrounded by whispering, hurrying obedience to his every whim, while beyond the swords and halberds which enclosed and protected him fresh dangers were for ever approaching; admired, feared, and hated by Europe writhing in torment and stunned by the thunder of war, but imperious to his last breath, he passed in pomp and suffering to his death.

CHAPTER XV

THE CONSPIRACY OF CINQ-MARS
—THE END

SINCE the king, after Mlle. de Lafayette had sought the cloister, was once more holding long conversations, by no means welcome to the Cardinal, with Mlle. de Hautefort, Richelieu, who was aware that masculine friendships appealed more strongly to the king, brought to the Court the young Marquis de Cinq-Mars, the son of his dead friend, the Maréchal d'Effiat. He attained his end only too surely; never yet had anyone so pleased the king; the Hautefort at once fell out of favour. The amiable, handsome young man, though not yet twenty years of age, was appointed to one of the highest positions at Court; he was made grand master of the horse. But the Court was a wearisome place, and Cinq-Mars liked to amuse himself; he rose late, instead of going hunting with the king in the early morning; he loved women; he pleased Marion Delorme and the lovely Princess Marie Gonzaga; and the king was jealous of women. There were quarrels and reconciliations between this curious pair of friends or lovers; they plighted their mutual troth in writing, declaring that they would remain good friends. The king's favour, which meant so much in those days, intoxicated the young man. He saw himself a duke or constable, like Luynes, and thought that he would then be able to marry the princess. Presently it began to displease him that the Cardinal, who saw in him the son of his friend, whom he had known as a little boy, and whom he had made what he was, should treat him now, as of old, as a young friend of no importance. He took it for granted that he must now take a hand in political affairs, but when one day he remained in the king's cabinet, and the Cardinal came to have audience, the latter sent him out of the room with the words: "Affairs of State are not discussed before children." Cinq-Mars was furious, but the Cardinal, too, began to lose his temper; there could be no talk, he told him, of marriage with the Princess Marie. The favourite began to scoff at the minister and his magnificence, and did not fail to note that this by no means displeased the king, that he laughed and sneered. He did not understand the duality of the king's nature. Louis, however, lent himself gladly to this distraction; it amused him, and their conversations became more and more hazardous. After all, said Cinq-Mars, he could with a word remove the man who caused him so much annoyance; could even have him put to death. The king's dangerous reply was that one must not kill a priest, a cardinal; it would be a deadly sin. In the king's service the captain of his musketeers was a resolute Gascon, M. de Troisville. When matters had got to this stage Cinq-Mars spoke to him. Murder, said the captain, was not really his business, but it would be if the king commanded him to make it so. And it pleased the king to think that he had the power to say: "There is a man who would kill even the Cardinal if I ordered him to do so." But he did not give the order.

Meanwhile Cinq-Mars was already meddling in high politics, without thinking of Chalais and the rest who had attempted to do so before him. Through the Vicomte de Fontrailles he had dealings with the Comte de Soissons and the Duc de Bouillon, who was preparing for insurrection in Sedan. And when Soissons fell so suddenly, Bouillon, while making his peace with the Cardinal, kept in touch with the rising star. Through the Comte d'Aubijoux and the Marquis de Montrésor, who after Puylaurens' death had become Monsieur's chamberlain, he invited Gaston to take a hand, and Gaston was once more ready to do so; Fontrailles assured him that the queen also was involved. In the Hôtel de Venise, in which Monsieur had his stables, he and Bouillon and Cinq-Mars met together; Fontrailles was sent with a draft of a treaty to Spain, and returned some time later with the treaty signed; Spain would supply the conspirators with troops against the Cardinal, in return for which peace was to be concluded on the basis of the *status quo ante*. What could have been more welcome to Olivarez, now that the military position had become so unfavourable to Spain? Fontrailles found the procedure tedious; he was all for a quicker method; Cinq-Mars was in agreement with him; they seem more than once to have laid their plans together. The Court in the meanwhile had begun a journey to the southern seat of war. In Lyons the murder is said to have been prevented by Gaston's irresolution. The Cardinal wrote later: "After this even the infernal demon intended to have me murdered in my bed at Narbonne." He suspected what was afoot, but he had no proof. He was then so seriously ill that he had to leave the Royal train and have himself carried to Tarascon. He could no longer use his right arm; it was covered with ulcers. The secretary of State, De Noyers, and Cardinal Mazarin, who since the death of Père Joseph had become his most important collaborator, remained with the Court. They transacted certain business with the Court, but when they had gone Louis XIII, as before, continued his hazardous conversations with his master of horse; again and again he declared that the Cardinal was indispensable, and kept beside him as a friend the man who wanted to have the Cardinal murdered. Meanwhile too many already knew of the affair. In Perpignan, Fontrailles saw a letter of the Princess Marie's to Monsieur, in which she wrote that all Paris was talking of his plans; and when he noticed that the king was shutting himself up with De Noyers and Chavigny, and holding long conferences with them, he became anxious. He warned Cinq-Mars, who paid no attention to him. "Well," he said, "you, after all, will be tall enough when the headsman has taken your head off your shoulders; I am too short already." Fontrailles was, indeed, short and hunchbacked; he escaped in the robe of a Capucin. The Cardinal had obtained, through a spy whom he kept in his pay at the Court of Madrid, a copy of the treaty, and bade Chavigny lay it before the king. As soon as the king realized that his favourite had not only jested pleasantly over the murder, but had also committed high treason, he unhesitatingly ordered his arrest, with that of his friend, the President de Thou, in whom Cinq-Mars had confided. The

Duc de Bouillon, who was with the army in Italy, was arrested at Casale and taken to Pinerolo. The king, as always, was skilfully handled; malevolent assertions which Cinq-Mars was said to have made were duly reported to him. In all Richelieu's indictments, however just his cause, there is a false, spiteful, unctuous tone; he would never have thought it possible, he wrote, that anyone would have sought to murder a cardinal, a priest, who for twenty-five years had given loyal service. . . . The king, who was himself grievously ill with rheumatism, had to return from Narbonne to Paris; and as he was passing Tarascon he visited the Cardinal. He went with a bad conscience. Lying on his bed, he had himself carried into Richelieu's chamber; and there they lay, both sick unto death, the king and his minister, facing one another on their beds. They were both very greatly agitated; the tears ran down their faces as they spoke; and Richelieu assured his "ever-gracious monarch" of his "eternal gratitude."

He enjoyed his revenge to the full. Carried on board a vessel on the Rhone, he had the President de Thou towed behind, in a second boat, to Lyons, to his execution. He was condemned under an old, forgotten statute, because he had not exposed the plot in which he had refused to participate. He and Cinq-Mars died on the scaffold in Lyons. The description of their last days and of the execution in Fontraille's narrative, of the agitation and exaltation of the nervous De Thou, and the theatrical bravery with which both men died, makes extraordinary reading. "I should like to know what sort of a face Monsieur the Grand

Master of the Horse is pulling now," said Louis XIII, at the hour fixed for the execution. He continually looked at the clock, until he knew that the heads had fallen. The Duc de Bouillon was saved by the protests of the Nassau and Hesse families, to whom he was related, and who, being allies of France, had to be treated with consideration; and also by his wife's threat to deliver the stronghold of Sedan to the Spaniards. But he was saved only on condition that he surrendered his principality to France. The other participants in the plot had fled. Monsieur, on the first news of the arrest, had written submissive letters to the king, the Cardinal, Mazarin, and Chavigny. "This ungrateful M. le Grand Écuyer," he wrote to Richelieu, "how guilty he is, who was under such obligations to you! I have always been on my guard against him and his intrigues; you, my cousin, have all my respect and friendship. . . ." But this did not help him for the moment; he was forced to go into exile, to Venice, and there he lived as a private person on an income of 10,000 thalers monthly. But as he once more confessed everything and betrayed everybody he was allowed to live in Blois, as duke; he was merely deprived of his guard of honour.

The Cardinal left Lyons the moment sentence was passed on Cinq-Mars and De Thou. From the banks of the Rhone his decaying, suffering body, since by reason of ulcers on the buttocks he could no longer sit, was conveyed to the Loire in a specially constructed litter with a violet cover, which was carried by four-and-twenty bearers. The walls of houses were torn open that he might be hoisted into his room as painlessly as might be; then a whole fleet of vessels descended the Loire, while squadrons of cavalry rode along either bank. The Duc d'Enghien, who had to play "the good nephew," had the sluices opened to admit water to the dried-up channels, in order to spare the sick man the pain of being carried by road. So the dying minister returned victorious to Paris. He insisted on the dismissal of Troisville, about whom he had begun to feel uneasy.

This was in October 1642. On the 4th of December he died. "Until his last sigh," says Monglat, "he retained that pride and majesty which he had displayed all his life." When the priest of Saint-Eustache, on giving him the last sacrament, asked him whether he forgave his enemies, he replied that he had never had any save the enemies of the State. Until his last hour he continued to send the secretaries of State to the king, and when the king himself came to visit him he spoke of affairs of State and of the war as though nothing was to be altered.

On the 23rd of May, in the castle of the Vicomtes of Narbonne, he had made his will. He had not been able to sign it with his disabled arm, so Cardinal Mazarin and other ecclesiastics and gentlemen had to sign it as witnesses. In this will he appointed as his heir-in-chief his grand-nephew, Armand de Vignerot, who became Duc de Richelieu and inherited most of the Cardinal's estates. His nephew, Armand de Brézé, inherited the dukedom of Fronsac, and the Duchesse d'Aiguillon the usufruct of the so-called Petit-Luxembourg, which belonged to him, and, in addition to a great deal of plate and jewellery, almost all the ready money which he left behind him; which, after paying his debts, she was to apply to works of piety, and which was very largely applied to the prosecution of countless lawsuits. One and a half million livres he left to the king, as a fund to be applied to political uses. Then followed a few dozen legacies, mostly to servants and employés of his family, and one or two thousand livres to Renaudot, the publisher of the *Gazette de France*.

"A great statesman is dead," said Louis XIII, when he received the news. And on the same day he called Mazarin, whom the dead man had recommended to him, to the head of the Government.

By the whole of Europe the Cardinal's death was regarded as an event of the greatest importance. Urban VIII, the ever-witty Pope, said: "If there is a God he will presumably have to make atonement; if there is no God he was a valiant man."

The Cardinal-Duke was borne with pomp to the grave; the catafalque, surrounded by the guard of honour, was exposed for many days. At the obsequies three thousand candles were lit in the church of Notre-Dame, which was hung all with black; and the funeral sermon was preached by the bishop of Sarlat, Jean de Lingendes, one of the best preachers in France. The dead Cardinal was buried in the church of the Sorbonne, which he himself had founded.

But at the same time the now liberated hatred of all those who had bowed their heads and ground their teeth found expression in rejoicing over the Cardinal's death, and in threats against the "creatures" and the relatives of the dead man, who sat in high places and

THE END

inherited his riches. "Now he is dead and put away" was the refrain of a song which was sung in every street, and sung, too, by the Bishop of Vannes, in the assembly of the Estates of Brittany, and in the face of the Maréchal de La Meilleraye.

Few understand the work of the dead man; all felt that they were freed of the burden of fear and oppression which had weighed upon the country. The prisons opened their doors; banished men and fugitives made ready for the homeward journey.

"One must let the storm wear itself out," said Mazarin. But the king retained Richelieu's kinsmen and servants in their offices, and carried out almost all his dispositions. By the appointment of Mazarin he ensured, as far as he could, the continuance of his policy.

He survived his minister only by a few months. The two men, who had held fast to one another, in a loveless friendship, out of a profound community of interests, fared together to the grave. The powers which Richelieu had held in subjection were not, indeed, destroyed; neither the old power of the feudal nobility nor the new power of bourgeois liberty. Both rose against his successor in the four years' revolution of 1648, but owing to the incapacity of their leaders his tenacious policy defeated them.

Richelieu, Mazarin, and Louis XIII were the creators of modern absolutism. Since Louis XIV had only the will and not the intellect of his predecessors, and was incapable of practising moderation as they had done, he pursued a policy of power which united all Europe against France. The first absolute monarch proved forthwith that absolutism is not an organization, but only a convenience for the rulers; that it will for a short time permit of an intense concentration and exploitation of all the energies of a nation, until these energies languish under it or destroy it.

This does not diminish the human phenomenon. What an indomitable and imperious will, combined with the keenest understanding and absolute coolness, can achieve, despite the stoutest opposition—this Richelieu has shown us.

INDEX

Aiguillon, *see* Vignerot
Albrecht, Archduke of Austria, 38
Aligre, Étienne d', 143
Althann, Count, 160
Aña, Dona, *see* Anne of Austria
Angoulême, Duc d', *see* Auvergne
Anne of Austria, Queen of France, 44, 50, 51, 62, 136-9, 141, 146, 154, 166, 216, 217, 218, 222
Arnoux, Père Jean, 86, 90, 102, 106
Aubijoux, François Jacques d'Amboise, Comte d', 235
Aumale, Claude de Lorraine, Chevalier d', 25
Aumont, Jean d', Marshal of France, 56
Auvergne, Charles de Valois, Comte d', Duc d'Angoulême, 66, 102, 154
Aytona, Marques d', 212

Ballouet (properly Boislouet), 212
Balzac, Jean Louis Guez de, 230
Banér, Johann, 191
Barberini, Francesco, Cardinal, 135
Barbin, Claude, 51, 52, 61, 64, 66, 75, 77, 80, 226
Bartolini, Tuscan envoy, 89
Basoche, The, 23
Bassompierre, François de, Marshal of France, 38, 75, 82, 98, 104, 137, 154, 157, 171, 173-4, 221
Baugy, N. de Bar, Seigneur de, 68
Beaumont, Hardouin de Péréfixe, Abbé de, 200
Beaumont, N. de, 224
Bellarmin, Robert, Cardinal, 30
Bellegarde, Roger de St. Lary, Duc de, 137, 167
Bentivoglio, Guido, Cardinal, 40, 65, 103, 108
Bérulle, Père Pierre de, 61
Bethlen, Gabor, 100
Béthune, Philippe de, Comte de Selles et Charost, 102
Bézé, Théodore de, 30
Biron, Armand Gontauld, Marshal of France, 34, 56
Bodin, Jean, 30
Boisrobert, François le Metel, Abbé de, 224-5, 230
Bon, Ottavio, 65

RICHELIEU

Borghese, Scipio Caffarelli, Cardinal, 86
Boucher, Jean, 30
Bouillon, Eleanore Cathérine Febronie de Bergh, Duchesse de, 238
Bouillon, Frédéric Maurice de La Tour d'Auvergne, Duc de, 210, 235, 236-8
Bouillon, Henri de La Tour d'Auvergne, Comte de Turenne, Duc de, 42, 44, 50, 51, 52, 65, 69, 84, 90, 101, 105, 114
Bourbon-Soissons, Comte de, *see* Soissons
Bouthillier, Claude de, 130-1, 209
Bouthillier, Léon de, *see* Chavigny
Brandenburg, Sigismund, Elector of, 40
Brantes, Léon d'Albert de, Duc de Luxembourg, 72
Brenne, Comte de, Master of Horse to Queen Marie, 93
Brienne, Henri Auguste de Loménie, Seigneur, later Comte, de La Ville aux Clercs, 52, 64, 196
Brisson, Barnabé, 25
Brosse, Jacques de, 102
Buckingham, George Villiers, Duke of, 110, 135, 138-40, 151, 153, 156, 157
Bullion, Claude, 197

Cadenet, Honoré d'Albert de, Duc de Chaulnes, 73
Cadillac, 93
Calvin, John, 200
Caraffa, Carlo, Cardinal, 54
Carlisle, James Hay, Earl of, 138
Carré, P. Hugo, 209
Catinat, Georges de, 217
Caussin, P. Nicolas, 210
Chalais, Henri de Talleyrand, Marquis de, 143, 144, 145, 220, 221, 235
Champaigne, Philippe de, 223
Champigny, Bochart de, 114
Chanteloube, Père, 214
Charles I, King of England, 68, 135, 138, 150, 176
Charles V, Emperor, 31, 35
Charles VIII, King of France, 35
Charles IX, King of France, 66
Charnacé, Baron de, 183
Charost, Louis de Béthune, Duc de, 226
Charpentier, 124, 224
Charré, 224
Châteauneuf, Charles de l'Aubespine, Marquis de, 86, 102, 174, 176, 177, 196, 216, 220, 221
Chatillon, Gaspard de Coligny, Duc de, Marshal of France, 187

INDEX

Chaulnes, Duc de, 84
Chavigny, Léon de Bouthillier, Comte de, 130-1, 163, 164, 196, 207, 209, 213, 236, 238
Chevreuse, Claude de Lorraine, Prince de Joinville, Duc de, 137, 138-9, 141, 219, 221
Chevreuse, Marie Aimée de Rohan, Duchesse de Luynes et de Chevreuse, 84, 137, 139, 141, 142, 143, 144, 145, 146, 147, 153, 157, 215-20
Cinq-Mars, Henri Coëffier Ruzé d'Effiat, Marquis de, 233-8
Citois, François, 224
Clara Isabella Eugenia, Infanta of Spain, 172, 211
Clément, Jacques, 30, 54
Clérembault, Louis de, 53
Cochère, Denys Bouthillier, Abbé de la, 89, 94, 103
Cœuvres, see Estrées
Coislin, Pierre César de Cambout-Pontchâteau, Marquis de, 228
Collalto, Ramboldo, Conte di, 161
Combalet, Antoine de Beauvoir du Rourre, M. de, 99, 169, 227
Concini, Concino, Marquis d'Ancre, Marshal of France, 42, 45, 51, 61, 65, 71-83, 85, 90, 106, 121, 129, 232
Concini, Leonora, see Dori
Condé, Charlotte Marguerite de Montmorency, Princesse de, 38, 142
Condé, Clémence de Maillé-Brézé, Princesse de, 177, 229
Condé, Henri II de Bourbon, Prince de, Duc d'Enghien, 38, 41, 45, 46, 49, 50, 51, 63, 74, 97, 101, 108, 122, 142, 144, 147-8, 177-8, 187, 210, 229
Condé, Louis II de Bourbon, Duc d'Enghien, Prince de, 193, 239
Conti, François de Bourbon, Prince de, 41, 42
Conti, Louise Marguerite de Lorraine, Princesse de, 41, 137, 168, 173
Cordoba, Don Gonsalvo de, 38, 159
Corneille, Pierre, 230, 231
Corsini, Monsignore, nuncio
Cotton, Father, 61
Cramail, Adrian de Montluc, Comte de, 221
Créqui, Charles Blanchefort de Bonne, Duc de, 171
Cromwell, Oliver, 32

Déagent, Guichard, 77, 78, 85
Delorme, Marion, 227, 233
Desmarets, Jean, de Saint-Sorlin, 208, 231
Dohna, Fabian, Oberstburggraf von, 100
Dori, Leonora, wife of Concini, Marquis d'Ancre, known as Galigaï, 43, 51, 73-4, 79, 80
Du Perron, Jacques Davy, Cardinal, 47, 58, 106
Du Plessis, Antoine, 54

RICHELIEU

Du Plessis, confidant of the Duc d'Épernon, 91, 93
Du Plessis, François, 53, 54
Du Plessis, Guillaume, 53
Du Plessis, Jacques, Bishop of Luçon, 53
Du Plessis, Louis, 53, 54
Duplessis-Mornay, Philippe, 44, 114
Du Vair, Guillaume, 52

Effiat, Antoine Coëffier, Marquis d', Marshal of France, 197, 233
Egmont, Juste d', 223
Elbène, Alexandre d', 213
Elbœuf, Duchesse de, *see* Vendôme
Elisabeth de Bourbon, Queen of Spain, 44, 125
Elissavide, Grabien, 186
Enghien, Duc d', *see* Louis Condé
Épernon, Jean Louis de Nogaret et de La Valette, Duc d', 39, 42, 46, 51, 84, 90, 91–5, 97, 122, 221
Épernon, *see* La Valette
Erlach, General von, 192
Eschaux, Bertrand d', Bishop of Bayonne
Estates, The, 46–7, 62
Estrées, François Annibal, Marquis de Cœuvres, Duc d', Marshal of France, 133, 221

Fancan, Dorval Langlois de, Abbé, 106, 151
Felipe, Don, 44
Ferdinand, Archduke of Austria, *see* Ferdinand II
Ferdinand II, Kaiser, 67, 68, 101, 104, 121, 162, 168, 180
Ferdinand III, Kaiser, 162, 180, 189
Feria, Don Gomez de Figueroa e Cordova, Duca de, 104
Fernando, Don, Infante of Spain, 186
Feuquières, Manassès de Pas, Marquis de, 183–4
Fontrailles, Louis d'Astarac, Vicomte de, 235, 237
Francis I, King of France, 17, 57
Friedrich V, Elector Palatine (the "Winter King"), 101, 104, 110
Fronsac, Armand de Maillé-Brézé, 228, 239
Fürstenberg, Count Wratislaw, 101

Gallas, Matthias, Comte de, 184
Gassion, Jean de, Marshal of France, 206
Ginetti, Cardinal, 191
Girard, Guillaume, 91
Givry, Cardinal de, 58
Gonzaga, Charles, *see* Nevers

INDEX

Gonzaga, Francis, Duke of Mantua and Montferrat, 67
Gonzaga, Maria Louisa, later Queen of Poland, 165, 191, 233
Gordes, Guillaume de Simiane, Marquis de, 212, 217
Gramont, Antoine, Comte de Guiche, later Duc de, Marshal of France, 229
Gratiollet, Jean, 186
Gregory XV, Pope, 108
Grimmelshausen, Hans Jakob Christoffel, 190
Grisons, the, 36, 69
Grotius, Hugo, 185
Guébriant, Jean Baptiste de Budes, Comte de, Marshal of France, 193
Guillard, President, 17
Guise, Charles de Lorraine, Duc de, 25
Guise, Charles de Lorraine, Duc de Mayenne et de, 42, 44, 66, 122, 175, 210
Guise, Henri I de Lorraine, Duc de, 41, 54
Guise, Henriette Cathérine de Joyeuse, Duchesse de
Gussoni, Vicenzo, 65
Gustavus, Adolphus, King of Sweden, 117, 164, 180–2, 188

Habsburgs, the, 35, 39, 102, 109, 111, 120, 181, 185, 193
Hallier, François du, de l'Hôpital, later Marshal of France, 143
Harcourt, Henri de Lorraine, Comte de, 229
Harlay, Achille de, 25
Hauranne, Jean Duvergier de, Abbé de Saint-Cyran, 39, 199–200
Hautefort, Marie d', later Duchesse de Schomberg, 209, 233
Henri III, King of France, 15, 18, 54, 56, 68
Henri IV, King of France, 15, 18, 25, 33, 36, 37, 38, 39, 41, 43, 55, 56, 57, 60, 66, 69, 100, 114, 120, 142, 175
Henrietta Maria, Queen of England, 113, 134, 138, 141, 150
Holland, Lord, 138, 141
Hôpital, Michel de l', Chancellor, 33
Horn, Gustavus, Count, 184
Hotman, François de, 30
Huguenots, The, 44, 56, 100, 109, 135

Jars, François de Rochechouart, Commander de, 217, 221
Jeannin, Pierre, 41, 45, 49, 50, 94, 102, 114, 145
Johann, Georg, Elector of Saxony, 133
Joinville, Prince de, 82
Joseph, Père, *see* Tremblay

Kinsky, Wilhelm, Count von, 184
Kremsmünster, Anton, Abbot of, 164

RICHELIEU

La Boderie, Matthieu Lefèvre de, 184
La Boetie, Étienne de, 30
La Broye, Baron de, 226
Lafayette, Louise Motier de, 209, 233
Laffemas, Isaac de, 224
La Force, Jacques Nompar de Caumont, Duc de, Marshal of France, 105, 176, 187
La Girardière, Philippe Messeau de, 55
La Marck-Lumay, Comte de, 37
La Meilleraye, Charles de La Porte, Duc de, Marshal of France, 228, 241
Lamormaini, Père Guillaume, 163
La Porte, Amador de, 228
La Porte, Charles, *see* La Meilleraye
La Porte, François de, 35
La Porte, Prince de, 217
La Porte, Suzanne de, *see* Richelieu
Larcher, President, 25
La Rochefoucauld, François, Cardinal de, 108
La Rochelle, Siege of, 105, 149–57
La Valette, Bernard de Nogaret d'Épernon, Cardinal de, 96, 144, 171, 176, 187, 191, 228
La Vieuville, Charles, Marquis de, 111–14
La Vrillière, Louis Raymond Philippeaux de, 196
Leffler, Swedish envoy, 184
Le Masle, Michel, 124, 224
Le Mercier, Jacques, 222, 223
Léon, Charles Brûlart de Silley, Abbé de Joyenval, Prior de, 163, 168
Leopold, Archduke of Austria, 111
Lesdiguières, François de Bonne, Duc de, Constable of France, 38, 50, 69, 105, 109, 133, 152, 173
Lesdiguières, Anne de Magdelaine, Duchesse de, 173
Le Tellier, Michel, 187
Lingendes, Jean de, Bishop of Sarlat, 240
Longueville, Cathérine Gonzaga, Duchesse de, 66
Longueville, Henri II, d'Orléans, Duc de, 50, 97, 142, 182
Lorraine, Charles IV, Duke of, 153, 175, 211, 215, 216, 220
Lorraine, Nicholas François de, 211
Louis, St., 20
Louis XI, King of France, 23
Louis XII, King of France, 36, 169
Louis XIII, King of France, 35, 39, 47, 62, 71, 72 *et seq.*, 80, 81, 100, 101, 102, 107, 111, 113, 125–9, 136–8, 140, 145–7, 170, 177, 185, 190, 208–10, 213, 220, 221, 237–8, 240, 241

INDEX

Louis XIV, King of France, 15, 16, 115, 116, 187, 198, 199, 202, 203, 219, 241
Louvois, François Le Tellier, Marquis de, 187
Louvre, The, 19
Ludovici, Vincenzio, 91
Luther, Martin, 200
Luxembourg, Duc de, 84
Luynes, Louis Charles d'Albert, Duc de, 72 *et seq.*, 76 *et seq.*, 84–99, 101, 103, 105–7, 111, 118, 129, 233
Luynes, Marie de, *see* Chevreuse

Maillé-Brézé, Nicole de Richelieu, Marquise de, 63, 228
Maillé-Brézé, Urbain, Marquis de, Marshal of France, 228
Malherbe, François de, 49, 230
Manchester, Henry Montague, Earl of, 153
Mangot, Claude, Seigneur de Villarceaux, 31, 32, 80
Mansfield, Ernst, Count, 134
Marescot, M. de, 133
Mariana, Padre Juan de, 30
Marillac, Louis de, Marshal of France, 174, 221
Marillac, Michel de, 98, 114, 143, 166, 171, 203
Marsillac, François de La Rochefoucauld, Prince de, 219, 221
Matthias, Emperor, 100
Mausson, M. de, 54
Maximilian I, Elector of Bavaria, 104, 180–1
Mayenne, Henri de Lorraine, Duc de, 50, 97
Mazarin (Mazarini), Giulio, Cardinal, 115, 129, 156, 161, 169, 178, 187, 192, 198, 232, 236, 238, 239, 241
Medici, Marie de', Queen of France, 39 *et seq.*, 45, 65, 73, 79, 81–2, 89–90, 93–8, 102, 107, 109, 123, 136, 138, 140, 165–172, 214, 217
Mercœur, Philippe Emmanuel de Lorraine, Duc de, 56
Mirabeau, G. H. V. Riquetti, Comte de, 108
Mirabel, Marquis de, 218
Miron, Robert, 47
Moisset, 222
Molé family, 25
Molière (Jean Baptiste Poquelin), 49
Monglat, François de Clermont, Marquis de, 239
Monglat, Jeanne de Harlay, Baronne de, 125
Monot, Père Pierre, 191
Montafié, *see* Soissons
Montague, Walter, 153, 154, 217
Montbazon, Ercule Rohan, Duc de, 84
Monteleone, Duke of, 65, 101

Montigny, François de la Grange de, Marshal of France, 66
Montluc, Blaise de, Marshal of France, 54, 145
Montmorency, Charlotte de, *see* Condé
Montmorency, Felicia Orsini, Duchesse de, 176
Montmorency, Henry I, Duc de, Constable, 38, 122
Montmorency, Henry II, Duc de, Marshal of France, 134, 137, 152, 175–7, 221
Montmorency-Boutteville, François, Comte de, 175
Montpensier, Anne Marie Louise d'Orléans, Duchesse de (Mademoiselle), 140
Montpensier, Marie de, *see* Orléans, 213
Montrésor, Claude de Bourdielle, Marquis de, 235
Morgues, *see* Saint-Germain

Neuburg, Philipp Ludwig, Count Palatine, 40
Nevers, Charles I, Gonzaga, Duke of Mantua and of Montferrat, 37, 42, 50, 63, 65, 66, 101, 142, 158, 164, 165, 169
Nostitz, M. de, 164
Nouveau, M. de, Director of Posts, 223
Noyers, François Sublet, Baron de, 196, 236

Olivarez, Don Gasparo de Guzman, Conde d', Duca de San Lucar de Barrameda, 217
Orange, Frederick Henry of, Prince of Nassau, 188
Orange, Maurice of, Prince of Nassau, 188
Orléans, Jean Baptiste Gaston de Bourbon, Duc d'Anjou et d' (Monsieur), 82, 122, 140, 142, 144, 145, 157, 165, 166, 170–2, 175–7, 200, 211–14, 220, 235
Orléans, Marguerite de Lorraine, Duchesse de (Madame), 211
Orléans, Marie de Montpensier, Duchesse de (Madame), 145
Ornano, Jean Baptiste d', Marshal of France, 79, 89, 142, 147
Oxenstjerna, Axel, 184–5, 190

Paris, 19
Parlements, The, 18–22
Pascal, Blaise, 230
Paul V, Pope, 58
Paul, Vincent de, 199
Pescara, Fernando Francesco d'Avalos, Marchese di, 35
Philip (II) Augustus, King of France, 19
Philip IV, King of Spain, 158, 219
Philippe le Bel, 19
Piccolomini, Ottavio, Comte, 169
Pluvinel, Antoine de, 57
Poerson, Charles, 223

INDEX

Pontchâteau, Mlle. de, 212
Pont-Courlay, François de, 228
Pont-Courlay, Françoise de Richelieu, Baronne de, 228
Pont-Courlay, Réné, Baron de, 57, 77, 88, 99, 228
Puylaurens, Antoine de Laage, Duc de, 212, 228
Puyzieux, *see* Sillery

Questenberg, Gerhard, Freiherr von, 164

Rákóczy, George I, 191
Ravaillac, François, 30
Renaudot, Théophraste, 229, 240
Retz, Henri de Gondi, Cardinal de, 107, 108
Retz, Jean François Paul de Gondi, Cardinal, 78, 215, 227
Richelieu, Alphonse de, 228
Richelieu, Armand de Vignerot, Duc de, 239
Richelieu, François (IV) Du Plessis, Seigneur de, 35
Richelieu, Françoise de, *see* Pont-Courlay
Richelieu, Henri, Marquis de, 57, 63, 88, 95, 228
Richelieu, Marguerite Guyot des Charmeaux, Marquise de, 88
Richelieu, Nicole de, *see* Maillé-Brézé
Richelieu, Suzanne de, *see* La Porte, 55
Richer, Edmond, 150
Rochechouart, Françoise de, 56
Rocheposay, Châteignier de la, Bishop of Poitiers, 59
Rohan, Marguerite de Béthune, Duchesse de, 142
Rohan, Marie Aimée de, *see* Chevreuse
Rohan-Gié, Henri I, Duc de, Prince de Léon, 42, 44, 49, 109, 134, 153, 157, 158, 188
Rossignol, Antoine, 224
Ruccellai, Luigi, Abbé, 90, 94, 95, 108
Rudolf, II, Emperor, 38

Saint-Cyran, *see* Hauranne
Saint-Evremond, Charles de Marguetel de St. Denis de, 230, 231
Saint-Georges, captain of the guard, 79, 130
Saint-Germain, Matthieu de Morgues, Abbé de, 214
Saint-Simon, Claude de Rouvroy, Marquis de, 172
Santarelli, Père Antonio, 149
Savaron, Jean, 47
Savelli, General, 192
Savoy, Charles Emmanuel I, Duke of, 67, 69, 133, 158, 161, 176
Savoy, Christine de Bourbon, Duchess of, 191, 192
Savoy, Maurice, Prince of, Cardinal, 191
Savoy, Thomas, Prince of, 191, 192

Savoy, Victor Amadeus I, Duke of, 178, 191
Schomberg, Henri de Nanteuil, Comte de, Marshal of France, 68, 89, 95, 111, 114, 134, 176, 196
Schomberg, Kaspar von, 68
Séguier, Pierre, 196, 206
Servien, Abel, Marquis de Sablé, 196, 209
Servin, Louis, 80
Sillery, Nicolas Brûlart de, 41, 102, 107
Sillery, Pierre Brûlart de, Vicomte de Puyzieux, 102, 103, 107
Soissons, Anne de Montafié, Comtesse de Bourbon, 41
Soissons, Charles de Bourbon, Comte de, 41, 42
Soissons, Louis de Bourbon, Comte de, 97, 122, 141, 142, 153, 210
Sötern, Johann Philipp von, Elector of Trier, 186
Soubise, Benjamin de Rohan, Baron de Frontenai, Prince de, 42, 134
Souvré, Gilles de, Marquis de Courtenvaux, Marshal of France, 73
Spada, Bernardino, Cardinal, 150
Spinola, Ambrogio, Marques de los Balbazes, 104, 134, 159, 161–2
States-General, The, 49
Suarez, Padre Francisco, 30
Suffren, Père Jean, 124, 174
Sully, Maximilian de Béthune, Baron de Rosny, Duc de, 34, 37, 38, 41, 42, 102

Tallemant des Réaux, Gedéon, 213
Tardif, Jean, 25
Tellier, 187
Thémines, Charles Pons de Lauzière, Marquis de, 95
Thomas, Aquinas, 200
Thou, François Auguste de, 236–7
Thurn, Heinrich Matthias, Count, 100
Tillières, Leveneur, Comte de, 141
Toiras, Jean de St. Bonnet, Comte de, Marshal of France, 152, 159
Toledo, Don Pedro de, 67
Tremblay, Charles le Clerc du, 88, 89, 224
Tremblay, François le Clerc du (Père Joseph), 59, 88, 94, 106, 112, 131, 155, 162, 170, 172, 180, 181, 183, 186, 189, 196, 198–9, 209, 224
Troisville (Tréville), Armand Jean de la Peyre, M. de, 234, 239
Turenne, Henri de La Tour d'Auvergne, Vicomte de, 193
Tuscany, Francis I, Grand Duke of, 89

Ubaldini, Roberto, Monsignore, nuncio, 40
Urban VIII, Pope, 185, 240

INDEX

Valençay, Adielle d'Étampes, Commander, 143
Va-nu-pieds, Jean, 206
Vautier, François, 174
Vendôme, Alexandre de, Grand Prior of France, 129, 142, 144, 147
Vendôme, César, Duc de, 41, 46, 71, 97, 98, 142, 144, 147
Vendôme, Henriette Cathérine de, Duchesse d'Elbœuf, 136, 173
Vignerot, Marie Madeleine, de Combalet, Duchesse d'Aiguillon, 227, 239
Villeroy, Nicolas de Neufville, Seigneur de, 41, 45, 80
Vincenti, Selvaggia, 60
Vitry, Nicolas de l'Hôpital, Duc de, Marshal of France, 78, 84, 97, 143, 221
Voiture, Vincent, 230
Vouet, Simon, 223

Wallenstein, (properly Waldstein), Wenzel Eusebius Albrecht von, Duke of Frieland, 159, 163, 180, 184
Weimar, Bernhard von, Duke of Saxony, 184, 188, 191–2
Werth, Johann von, 192

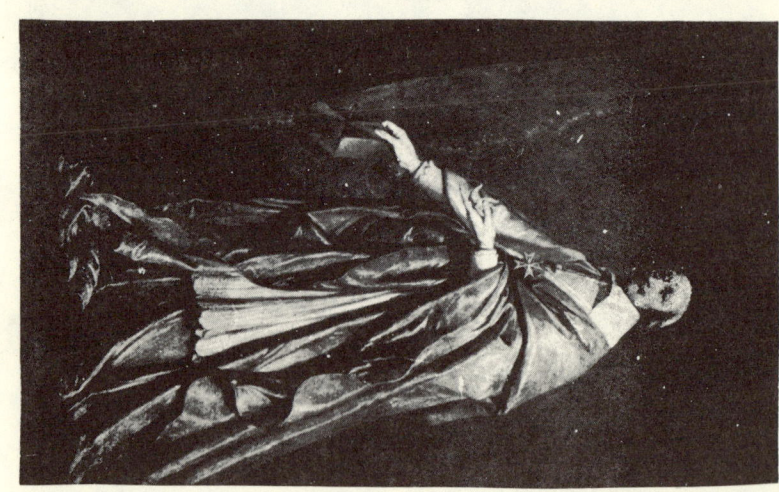

MAZARIN
(Philippe de Champaigne. *Portion of painting, Musée Condé, Chantilly*)

RICHELIEU
(Philippe de Champaigne. *Louvre, Paris*)